COCKTAILS AT DINNER

DARING PAIRINGS OF DELICIOUS DISHES AND ENTICING MIXED DRINKS

by *Michael Turback*

★ *and* ★

Julia Hastings-Black

Skyhorse Publishing

Skyhorse Publishing books may be purchased in bulk at special discounts for sales promotion, corporate gifts, fund-raising, or educational purposes. Special editions can also be created to specifications. For details, contact the Special Sales Department, Skyhorse Publishing, 307 West 36th Street, 11th Floor, New York, NY 10018 or info@skyhorsepublishing.com.

Skyhorse® and Skyhorse Publishing® are registered trademarks of Skyhorse Publishing, Inc.®, a Delaware corporation.

Visit our website at www.skyhorsepublishing.com.

10 9 8 7 6 5 4 3 2 1

Library of Congress Cataloging-in-Publication Data is available on file.

Cover design by Owen Corrigan

Print ISBN: 978-1-62914-523-5
Ebook ISBN: 978-1-62914-906-6

Printed in China

CONTENTS

INTRODUCTION

"My rule of life prescribed the drinking of alcohol before, after, and if need be, during all meals and in the intervals between them."

— Winston Churchill

★ ★ ★ ★ ★

To state the obvious before getting into the curious, wine has long been the indispensable companion to fine dining. But curiously, as the profession of bartender becomes more like that of a chef, collaboration between bar and kitchen has progressed. "The marriage of food and wine should allow for infidelity," suggested culinary writer Roy Andries de Groot. Ingredient-driven cocktails, made with top-shelf liquors, fresh seasonal fruits, flavored bitters, and other artisanal components, have begun to reflect a restaurant's artful cuisine and to challenge wine's dominance as the dinner beverage of choice. The secret is out—our food is having an affair with cocktails.

The mutual attraction of cocktails and food was noticed as early as 1933 in the book *What'll You Have?* by Julien J. Proskauer: "The perfect hostess never serves cocktails without some little appetizer accompanying them." This book explores cocktail pairings beyond the traditional accompaniments. Forty-four original pairings, including appetizers, soups, salads, entrées, and desserts were collected from restaurants around the United States.

First-rate food and mixed drinks—judiciously and harmoniously paired—become something more than the sum of their parts. *Cocktails at Dinner* serves as a primer to these progressive combinations for the home kitchen and bar, for cooks and bartenders at all levels. It showcases a range of innovative, yet accessible recipes from a diversity of cuisines, opening the door to new possibilities in dining and entertaining.

This compendium is a coming out of sorts for a restless band of artisans who have in common the desire to deliver something more and the willingness for open exchange. An idea may originate in the kitchen and then work its way out to the bar. Or a bartender's novel concoction might provide inspiration for a new dish by the chef. Parisian bartender Colin Peter Field suggests that, "like great sauce chefs, bartenders must be experienced and thoughtful as far as their ingredients are concerned." The joint efforts of chefs and bartenders featured here provide unexpected pleasures and stretch palate perspectives. The process or methodology by which each pairing came together is explained, leading the reader on a sensorial journey to new and interesting partnerships at the table.

Cocktails can lend a more festive atmosphere to special occasions, and playing matchmaker with food and drink could liven up the menu at your next get-together. Successful pairings require familiarity with the flavors and aromas of spirits and liqueurs, as well as an understanding of food preparations, ingredients, and the ways different flavors harmonize and connect. For you, dear reader, we offer a book's worth of examples and guidance. With this volume as trusted accomplice, you'll be able to recreate a variety of enlightened pairings with precision and confidence.

PAIRING PRINCIPLES

★ ★ ★ ★ ★

Like jazz, a successful pairing can't always be explained in specifics, but you know it when you taste it. The flavors and textures of a well-paired dish and drink will play off of each other in surprising and pleasing ways. Sometimes a cocktail works so well with a dish, you can't imagine one without the other. When experimenting with new pairings, begin by tasting each in your mind. If food drives the cocktail, consider the dish's flavor profiles and then fashion a complementary drink. If a cocktail inspires a counterpart from the kitchen, find a proper balance, with neither food nor drink dominating the other.

The Italian sartorial art of contrasting jackets and trousers is called *spezzato*, a term we have appropriated from menswear to describe a food/cocktail pairing gone wrong. The benefits of experimentation are undeniable, yet one should avoid a *spezzato* at the dinner table like a mismatched top and bottom. The following principles are intended to inspire and guide your own successful matchmaking:

- Buy fresh, high-quality ingredients for both dish and cocktail. Professional mixologists build their drinks from the same pool of ingredients used by the chef.
- A cocktail pairs well with a dish by one of two means—matching or contrasting its flavors. For example, the smoky, woody flavor of a bourbon-based drink heightens similar flavors in barbequed meat. On the flipside, a cocktail can temper extreme flavors— for example, a sweet or fruit-driven drink can bring a cool contrast to a spicy dish.
- Complement a dish by using a common ingredient (or ingredients) in the cocktail recipe. Herbs can be used in this capacity, either muddled or added as garnish for their aroma and visual appeal.
- If a cocktail's predominant flavors come from the mixers, rather than the spirits, use those to guide the pairing. For instance, the lemon in a margarita instead of the tequila might better define a partnership with a seafood dish.

- For a dish with complicated flavors or multiple seasonings, serve a cocktail that's simple and distinct. Don't overpower the dish.
- Avoid pairing a high-alcohol cocktail with a dish that has especially subtle flavors. On the other hand, dishes with strong flavors such as fried foods or those containing cheese or smoked fish, can stand up to the taste of alcohol.
- Consider the texture or consistency of a cocktail. Thicker cocktails made with liqueurs are awkward with red meat or rich sauces. Frozen cocktails can overwhelm the palate, while carbonated cocktails pair well with full-flavored foods. A cocktail can reflect a textural element of the dish by incorporating spices and herbs.
- A dish paired with a cocktail may need more acidity than if it were paired with wine. Fatty or salty foods pair best with cocktails high in acidity. Salinity can tire the palate. Acidity enlivens, cleanses, and balances.
- For the dessert course, a cocktail should be sweeter than the dessert. Pay attention not only to flavor, but also to mouthfeel. Consider a full-bodied cocktail for the end of the meal, just as you might serve a cordial.
- Serve cocktails in small portions if pairings are offered with multiple courses.

MENU OF MIXED DRINKS AND DISHES

★ ★ ★ ★ ★

Small Plate Pairings

What's Your Twenty?
    +Tempura Eggplant Chips
Barley's Ghost
    +Lamb Pintxos with Harissa
35-MM Manhattan
    +Duck Confit with Blue Cheese and
    Huckleberry Gastrique
Pisco Sour
    +Sea Bass "Tiradito"
Ward Eight
    +Grilled Watermelon and Heirloom
    Tomato Salad
Amareno Trois
    +Sirloin Carpaccio
Herbaceous Tequila Bramble
    +Prawn Ceviche with Crostini
Mexican Brush Fire
    +Oven-Roasted Oysters with Chili-Tequila
    Butter
Juniper's Twist
    +Escolar-Stuffed White Mushrooms
The Last Word
    +"Still Life" with Garden Tomatoes,
    Ricotta, Crispy Chicken Skin, and Basil

Better Living
    +Cucumber Salad with Strawberries and
    Grilled Ricotta Salata
Savannah Spoken Word
    +Snapper Crudo with Juniper-Infused
    Butter
The Whiskey Shiver
    +Roasted Sweet Potatoes with Gremolata
    and Pepper Jam
The Sunday Morning
    +Blue Corn Hushpuppies with Voodoo
    Dipping Sauce
Right up My Alley
    +Lamb Tartare with Celery Root Remoulade
Red Wedding
    +Sweet Onion Soup with Bone Marrow
    Dumplings
Sazerac
    +Calf Sweetbreads with Dumplings
Cane Salato
    +Grilled Escarole "Sotto Aceti"
Disco Volante
    +Thai-Style Chicken Wings
Nightshade
    +Escabeche de Pescado in Avocado Cups

Rouge
+Truffle Popcorn with Pecorino Romano Cheese

Main Plate Pairings

Apples to Apricot
+Seared Maine Sea Scallops with Sweet Corn Soup
The Wilbur Mary
+Bison Burger with Charred Tomato Barbeque Sauce
Fireside 75
+Bourbon-Glazed Chicken & Waffles
Sarsaparilla Old Fashioned
+Yak Meatloaf with Chipotle Mashed Potatoes
The Brandy Bishop
+Veal Tournedos Chantal
Tongue Tied
+Salt & Pepper Wood-Fired Pork Ribs with Saba
Braised Pineapple-Vanilla Martini
+Cavatelli with Broccoli Rabe, Anchovy & Spicy Peppers
The Witch
+Vermouth-and-Fennel Steamed Mussels
Corpse Reviver #2.1
+Grilled Lamb Skewers with Garlic Mint Yogurt and Tomato Marmalade
New Cuban
+Jumbo Scallops with Roasted Red Pepper Chimichurri

Johnny's Appleseed
+Pork Mignon with Brussels Sprouts and Fingerling Potatoes
Morte Rossa
+Polenta Terra e Mare
Little Mr. Sunshine
+Potato Pierogi with Citrus Lavender Marmalade
Highbury Cocktail
+Flounder "Muffuletta"
"Breakfast in Denver" Bloody Mary
+Freakin' Denver Omelet
The Playboy
+Plantain Polenta with Spicy Tomato Ragu
All Hands on Deck
+Grilled Jerk Quail with Banana Rum Jam
Pimm's Blue Ribbon
+Skate Wing Fish & Chips

Dessert Pairings

Lavender Bee's Knees
+Lavender Goat Cheese Tartlets
Smoked Peach Manhattan
+Southern Peach Cobbler
The Lonely Hunter
+Chocolate-Banana-Nut Trifle
Bella Lugosi's Dead
+Orange Cardamom Chocolate Financiers
Elephant Flip
+Crème Fraiche Cheesecake

SMALL PLATE PAIRINGS

The Rosebud team worked in perfect unison to create an interesting dining experience, challenging the diner's notion of how food and cocktails could relate. "I like to think of my cooking as very approachable," says Chef Ron Eyester, "yet I want to convey a sense of depth. You usually will not find more than three or four different flavors on any of my plates." Ron chose eggplant as the focal point of the dish and called in Jeff Jackson, resident drinksmith and "wine dude" to work on a compatible cocktail. With his experience both in the

kitchen and behind the bar, Jeff's approach was methodical. "Coming from a wine background, I wanted to use a riff of the champagne cocktail, but with the fried dish I needed higher alcohol. Ron suggested a bold, smokey note, so I added a well-aged scotch to the recipe along with lime and orgeat in a kind of tantalizing tart/sweet dance. Distinctive as it was pleasurable, the cocktail came to life alongside the dish."

WHAT'S YOUR 20?
PAIRED WITH
TEMPURA EGGPLANT CHIPS

ROSEBUD, ALTANTA, GA
JEFF JACKSON, MIXOLOGIST
RON EYESTER, CHEF

The eggplant is a thing of beauty. Its ability to balance multiple flavors makes the vegetable a perfect complement to any meal involving several ingredients, and according to Mr. Eyester, its own mild flavor broadens the space for a range of influences. "Fried and crunchy foods pair well with high-intensity cocktails," explains the chef, whose beer-batter tempura meets its match with Mr. Jackson's complex drink.

WHAT'S YOUR 20?

MAKES 1 SERVING

The name is slang for "what's your location?" or "identify your position," a sly reference to the point at which a combination of ingredients is successful. The drinksmith begins with an aromatic Scotch, slightly sweet and fruity, with vanilla notes. It mixes well with the creamy texture of champagne liqueur, tartness of lime, and rich almond of orgeat. Complex yet drinkable—flavors and aromas bleed into one another.

★ ★ ★ ★ ★

1 ½ ounce Glenlivet 12-Year-Old Single Malt Scotch Whiskey
¾ ounce Henri Giraud Ratafia de Champagne
½ ounce freshly pressed lime juice
½ ounce orgeat syrup

Combine all ingredients with ice in a shaker. Shake vigorously and strain into a pre-chilled coupe.

TEMPURA EGGPLANT CHIPS

MAKES 4 SERVINGS

The chef uses this easy and clever technique to fry eggplants—sliced into chips, coated in batter, and dropped into searing hot oil so they cook quickly for an extra-crispy tempura crust. The cocktail is an excellent partner, stimulating the appetite with its "incense" and heightening the eggplant's flavors. Tempura is best served immediately and can be garnished with crumbled feta or goat cheese, and if you wish, a side of a favorite dipping sauce.

★ ★ ★ ★ ★

1 (12-ounce) bottle lager beer
3 cups tempura flour + flour for coating
8 cups soda water
1 teaspoon granulated garlic
1 tablespoon salt
1 large eggplant, peeled and cut into ½-inch slices
chopped parsley, for garnish
crumbled feta cheese, for garnish

Combine the beer, tempura flour, soda water, granulated garlic, and salt into a bowl. Mix to create tempura batter. Dip slices of eggplant into bowl of flour before dipping into the tempura batter. Cover the eggplant chip completely before frying. Fry at 350°F until golden brown, about 4 minutes on each side. Remove from the oil with a slotted spoon onto a plate lined with a paper towel (to absorb excess oil). Garnish with the parsley and feta cheese, and serve immediately.

What's Your 20? and Tempura Eggplant Chips

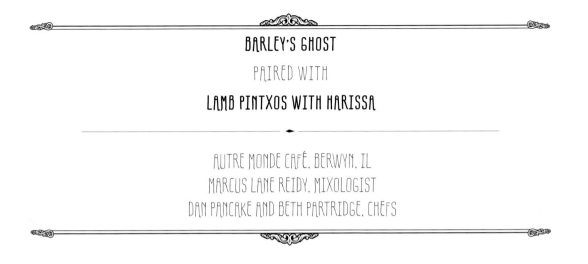

BARLEY'S GHOST

PAIRED WITH

LAMB PINTXOS WITH HARISSA

AUTRE MONDE CAFÉ, BERWYN, IL
MARCUS LANE REIDY, MIXOLOGIST
DAN PANCAKE AND BETH PARTRIDGE, CHEFS

In the Northern Basque region in Spain, *pintxos* (pronounced "peen-tchos") are the region's answer to tapas—skewered bites of grilled meats and veggies (the term comes from the verb *pinchar*, meaning to skewer or puncture). Usually eaten in local bars, these sociable dishes are rooted in the tradition of sharing food with friends. At Autre Monde, kitchen and bar take on the art of pintxos with grilled lamb, fired-up with Tunisian hot chili, and set into play with a seductive cocktail.

BARLEY'S GHOST

MAKES 1 SERVING

Orgeat (pronounced "or-zsa," like Zsa Zsa Gabor) syrup is made from almonds but was originally derived from barley water, according to food historian Ray Sokolov, and was an extraction of raw barley sweetened with sugar. The cocktail's reference point, an ingredient Sokolov calls "barley's ghost," adds texture, almond flavors, and nutty aromas to Mr. Reidy's composition. Oak-aged rum provides bittersweet, maple-like notes, and Crema's mescal-agave mix works its smoky-spicy magic in partnership with the spicy lamb dish.

★ ★ ★ ★ ★

1 ¼ ounces Zaya Gran Riserva
¾ ounce Small Hands Orgeat (almond syrup)
½ ounce Del Maguey Crema
¾ ounce freshly pressed lime juice
2 dashes Angostura bitters

Combine all ingredients with ice in a shaker. Shake vigorously and double-strain into a pre-chilled coupe. Serve without garnish.

LAMB PINTXOS WITH HARISSA

MAKES 8 SERVINGS

Pintxos provide an opportunity for imagination and creativity. There are no set rules—the goal is to create something flavorful and fun to eat. Skewers of succulent lamb with a sauce of sweet, piquant Piquillo peppers provide an attractive counterpoint to the cocktail. (The chef recommends metal skewers for grilling; wooden skewers must be soaked in water ahead of time and can be a bit messier.)

★ ★ ★ ★ ★

For the harissa spice:

1 tablespoon cumin
1 tablespoon coriander
¼ tablespoon cayenne
salt, to taste
black pepper, freshly cracked, to taste

Blend all spices together, and store in a sealed jar away from light.

For the harissa sauce:

10 whole Piquillo peppers (or other mild red peppers), roasted
1 tablespoon harissa spice (from above)
1 cup (approx.) olive oil

Combine roasted peppers and harissa spice in a blender and slowly add olive oil until it reaches a smooth consistency.

For the dish:

2 pounds lamb shoulder, ground
¼ cup half & half
4 tablespoons harissa spice (from above)
harissa sauce (from above)
mixed olives, roughly-chopped, for garnish
fresh cilantro, for garnish

Mix lamb, half & half, and harissa spice together in a large bowl. Form 2 ounces of lamb around each skewer in an oblong shape so that meat thickness is about ½ inch in the center of the skewer and ¼ inch at the bottom (two per skewer). Heat a charcoal grill to medium heat. Cook skewers directly on grill for about 4 minutes on each side or until meat gently springs back when pressed. Serve with harissa sauce, olives, and cilantro.

35-MM MANHATTAN

PAIRED WITH

DUCK CONFIT WITH BLUE CHEESE AND HUCKLEBERRY GASTRIQUE

TASTE RESTAURANT & BAR
(AT THE SEATTLE ART MUSEUM)
DUNCAN CHASE, MIXOLOGIST
CRAIG HETHERINGTON, CHEF

Confit came about centuries ago because of a practical need to preserve meat for long periods of time without refrigeration. In Chef Hetherington's kitchen, duck legs are cured with salt and then gently cooked in their own fat, emerging flavorful and tender. The succulent dish is paired with a vibrant cocktail created in 2012 for the thirty-fifth anniversary of the Seattle Art Museum's Film Noir series and named for 35-MM, the film gauge most commonly used for motion pictures.

35-MM Manhattan and Duck Confit with Blue Cheese and Huckleberry Gastrique

35-MM MANHATTAN

MAKES 1 SERVING

Oaky and smoky, Bulleit Bourbon is produced with a high rye content. It provides a spicy interplay with the anise, fennel, and angelica notes of the dry vermouth. Sherry adds hints of maple syrup, brown sugar, and plum jam to this twist on a Bourbon Manhattan in a wave of vigorous flavors that cut through the fatty glory of confit.

★ ★ ★ ★ ★

2 ounces Bulleit Bourbon
½ ounce Noilly Pratt Vermouth
½ ounce Lustau Solara Sherry
dash Fee Brothers Aztec Chocolate bitters
Orange twist garnish

Combine ingredients in a mixing glass with ice cubes. Stir and strain into a cocktail glass and garnish with an orange twist.

DUCK CONFIT WITH BLUE CHEESE AND HUCKLEBERRY GASTRIQUE

MAKES 6 SERVINGS

While modern society has mostly lost the need to preserve meat for months, it has not lost its taste for duck confit. Preparation is similar to maceration, but instead of infusing booze with fruit, you're infusing meat with fat and flavor. Among the cocktail's many flavors, it is the balanced, refreshing sherry more than any other ingredient that defines the partnership. Its aromatic notes of dates, prunes, and figs merge well with the salty cheese and the fruity gastrique.

★ ★ ★ ★ ★

For the polenta:

1 quart whole milk
¼ cup unsalted butter
1 cup fine polenta
salt

In a medium sauce pot, heat the milk and butter over medium heat until it just comes to a boil. Turn heat to low and slowly whisk in the polenta. Continue to cook and stir the polenta for 5 to 7 minutes, until the polenta is soft to the taste. Add salt to taste. Serve immediately.

For the gastrique:

2 cups white wine
1 cup white balsamic vinegar
2 cups huckleberries
1 cup white sugar

In a non-reactive sauce pan, combine all ingredients over medium-high heat. Once it comes to a full boil, turn the heat to low, stirring occasionally. Reduce the liquid until it becomes a syrupy consistency, which may halve the original volume. This will take about 30 minutes.

For the duck confit:

6 duck hindquarters (legs)
4 cups duck fat
2 tablespoons dry lavender
¼ cup kosher salt
¼ cup fresh rosemary sprigs
parchment paper
polenta (from above)
gastrique (from above)
1 cup crumbled blue cheese

Prep (one day before cooking): Lay the duck legs on a tray and sprinkle evenly with the salt and the lavender. Wrap with plastic wrap and let sit in the refrigerator overnight.

Preheat the oven to 220°F. In a medium-sized pot, melt the duck fat over low heat until it reaches 250°F. In a small roasting pan, sprinkle the rosemary sprig evenly along the bottom and arrange the duck legs so they fit snugly in one layer. Carefully pour the melted duck fat over the legs until as covered as possible. Cut the parchment paper to the size of the pan and lay it on top of the legs, while being careful to not get the hot fat on your fingers. Using a spoon, push the legs around so the duck fat is evenly incorporated. Cover with foil and cook for 2 to 2½ hours. Remove from the oven and transfer legs, skin-side down, to a warmed non-stick pan. Brown the skin until crispy.

To serve, spoon the polenta into four shallow bowls and sprinkle with the crumbled blue cheese. Place the duck confit on top and drizzle the huckleberry gastrique around the polenta or in a separate dipping dish on the side.

PISCO SOUR
PAIRED WITH
SEA BASS "TIRADITO"

PICCA, LOS ANGELES, CA
JULIAN COX, MIXOLOGIST
RICARDO ZARATE, CHEF

Pisco is a bright, flavorful brandy made from grapes cultivated along the coastal valleys of Peru. It provides the critical component in a cocktail invented by Victor Vaughn Morris, an American bartender who left the Prohibition-era United States to open a saloon in Lima. His Peruvian version of a Whiskey Sour has become the country's national drink.

PISCO SOUR

MAKES 1 SERVING

Gentleman's Companion author Charles Baker Jr. called it "South America's most famous and original mixed drink." The Pisco Sour is tart yet sweet, seemingly mild, yet deceptively potent. Citrus and simple syrup tame the brandy's strong spirit, and egg white foam adds a silky mouthfeel, while aromatics of bitters and cinnamon stimulate the appetite.

★ ★ ★ ★ ★

½ ounce simple syrup
⅜ ounce freshly squeezed lemon juice
(chilled)
⅜ ounce freshly squeezed lime juice
(chilled)
¾ ounce Pisco brandy
½ egg white
dash Angostura bitters
dash cinnamon tincture*

Prepare the simple syrup and refrigerate until ready to use. Add lemon juice, lime juice, Pisco, and simple syrup into a cocktail shaker, and shake vigorously without ice. Add the egg white and shake, long and hard, and strain into a pre-chilled coupe. There should be at least ½ inch of foam at the top. Add dashes of Angostura and cinnamon tincture.

*To make cinnamon tincture, simply fill a jar with several sticks of cinnamon, and then top with a high-proof neutral grain spirit and allow to sit for a week or more.

SEA BASS "TIRADITO"

MAKES 4 SERVINGS

The influence of the Japanese immigrants, who came to South America in the nineteenth century, shows in the way the fish is sliced rather than chopped, and why ginger, soy, and other Japanese ingredients appear in the traditional Peruvian "tiradito." Pairing with the Pisco cocktail, in the words of the Peruvian-born chef, "adds an interesting contrast to the richness of the tiradito that is almost shocking, in the most pleasant way."

★ ★ ★ ★ ★

20 ounces sushi-grade sea bass filet (cleaned)
1 pound red yams (or sweet potatoes)
4 tablespoons sugar
4 cinnamon sticks
1 teaspoon ginger, peeled and finely grated into paste
1 teaspoon garlic, peeled and finely grated into paste
¼ cup sesame oil
¼ cup olive oil
2 tablespoons soy sauce
½ teaspoon cilantro, julienned

Slice sea bass filet into 20 sashimi slices (to yield thin 1-ounce slices approximately 1 by 2 inches). Boil yam with sugar and cinnamon sticks in a quart of water until cooked. Pass cooked yam through a food mill to form a purée. On each of four plates, lay five slices of sea bass horizontally and evenly spaced. Rub them with ginger and garlic pastes. Heat sesame and olive oil until they begin to smoke, and carefully pour just enough over the sea bass to sear the surface. Drizzle soy sauce over the top and garnish with cilantro. Serve with the yam purée.

WARD EIGHT
PAIRED WITH
GRILLED WATERMELON AND HEIRLOOM TOMATO SALAD

IRVING STREET KITCHEN, PORTLAND, OR
MICHAEL GALLUCCIO, MIXOLOGIST
SARAH SCHAFER, CHEF

Boston legend holds that a certain cocktail was named in honor of Martin Lomasney, political boss of the city's eighth ward and a well-known prohibitionist. Lomasney probably never sampled the drink himself. This vintage tipple provides unexpected consort when it comes to the salad. Bright, fruit flavors on the plate pair well with bright, fruit flavors in the glass— refreshingly direct and to the point.

WARD EIGHT

MAKES 1 SERVING

The cocktail is similar to the reliable Whiskey Sour, with the substitution of grenadine syrup for sugar and the addition of orange juice. The brash nature of straight rye whiskey (Mr. Galluccio pours Old Overholt) in the Ward Eight is soothed with lemon and orange, and sweetened with pomegranate-based grenadine—without completely losing its identity.

★ ★ ★ ★ ★

2 ounces rye whiskey
¾ ounce grenadine
½ ounce fresh-squeezed lemon juice
¼ ounce fresh-squeezed orange juice
1 slice orange (in half-moon shape),
for garnish
1 cocktail cherry, for garnish

Combine the rye, grenadine, lemon juice, and orange juice with ice in a shaker. Shake vigorously and double strain into a pre-chilled cocktail glass. Garnish with orange and cherry on a toothpick.

GRILLED WATERMELON AND HEIRLOOM TOMATO SALAD

MAKES 4 SERVINGS

Ms. Schafer's dish is much more than a leafy palate cleanser. It's a fabulously composed salad whose flavors and textures complement those of the cocktail. Champagne vinegar, less acidic than other vinegars, produces a mellow dressing for a dish with lots of "bridge" ingredients and sweet notes in common with the drink.

★ ★ ★ ★ ★

For the vinaigrette:

¼ cup of red pepper jelly
⅓ cup of champagne vinegar
½ cup of vegetable oil
salt, to taste

Combine the red pepper jelly with the champagne vinegar. Using a whisk, slowly incorporate the oil until the dressing is emulsified. Taste for salt, adding a little if necessary.

For the salad:

1 small seedless watermelon
4 medium-size, ripe heirloom tomatoes,
cut into ¼-inch slices
1 bunch basil
1 bunch mint
¼ pound watercress or arugula
2 balls fresh mozzarella or Burrata
sea salt
black pepper, to taste

Cut each end of the watermelon to expose the flesh and slice it in half, setting the large cut side against the cutting board. Working around the melon, use a knife to cut off the rind, until you have made a hemisphere of rindless melon. Square the melon into a block, and slice into planks about ½-inch thick. Brush the planks of watermelon with a layer of the dressing, and let marinate in the fridge for about 15 minutes. On a hot grill, place a plank of marinated watermelon across the grates. Let sear for a minute or so, until char appears. Turn the melon 90 degrees, to achieve even grill marks. Remove and chill.

To serve, arrange a few tomato slices on each plate, seasoning each slice with a pinch of sea salt and black pepper. Cut the watermelon into squares, then into triangles, so each plate has two slices. Slice the mozzarella and lay over the top of each plate. In a small mixing bowl, dress the watercress or arugula with the vinaigrette. Place a small amount of dressed greens on top of each salad. Finish with picked basil and mint leaves. Serve immediately.

AMARENA TROIS

PAIRED WITH

SIRLOIN CARPACCIO

MOOO RESTAURANT, BOSTON, MA
MELISSA CONE, MIXOLOGIST
DAVID HUTTON, CHEF

Renaissance painter Vittore Carpaccio combined the precision of Dutch painting with the vibrant color of the Venetian masters, and the use of red in his paintings inspired a classic antipasto platter of sliced raw beef. In this steakhouse kitchen-bar collaboration, paper-thin sirloin is dressed with dark cherries and blue cheese. It is offered with a muscular, fruit-driven cocktail that amplifies the customary alliance of red meat and red wine.

AMARENA TROIS

MAKES 1 SERVING

Ms. Cone's atmospheric formula is evocative of a French 75, the cocktail named for a French artillery cannon. Red wine, with concentrated notes of dark cherry, is spiked with a deliciously fruity cognac, while the bubbles in sparking Brut Rosé tease aromatics from cherry bitters. Amarena Trois refreshes the palate after every bite of sirloin, leaving you ready for more.

★★★★★

1 Amarena cherry, muddled
½ ounce full-flavored red wine
2 ounces cognac
2 dashes cherry bitters
⅛ ounce simple syrup
Brut Rosé Champagne, to top
1 fresh cherry, coated with sugar,
frozen

Combine the muddled cherry, red wine, cognac, cherry bitters, and simple syrup with ice in a shaker. Shake vigorously and double-strain into a pre-chilled martini glass. Top with Brut Rosé Champagne. Garnish with the frozen cherry.

SIRLOIN CARPACCIO

MAKES 4 SERVINGS

French philosopher Roland Barthes wrote: "To eat steak rare represents both a nature and a morality." The nexus of sweet cherries, salty cheese, and hot horseradish provides bite and complexity without overpowering the sirloin. "For an antipasto, you want something to entice the palate," explains Mr. Hutton. "Awaken it a little bit."

★ ★ ★ ★ ★

12 ounces prime sirloin steak
(completely trimmed, fat cap off)
2 tablespoon grated fresh horseradish
4 tablespoons extra virgin olive oil
4 ounces Amarena cherries in syrup
1 ounce blue cheese
sea salt
black pepper, freshly ground
arugula leaves, for garnish

Place sirloin in freezer for 1½ to 2 hours so that it is firm enough to slice. Starting from the smaller side, slice the meat as thin as possible (paper thin), arranging slices around a large, pre-chilled plate or platter. Sprinkle with the freshly grated horseradish, and season with salt and pepper, to taste. Dress the cherries and syrup around the plate, and garnish with the arugula leaves. Drizzle the olive oil over the top, and finish with crumbles of the blue cheese.

Note: The restaurant uses an electric deli slicer to get ultra thin slices. If your kitchen is without this device, hand-slice the meat as thinly as possible, then gently pound out between two sheets of plastic wrap with a meat-tenderizing hammer. Keep covered before serving.

HERBACEOUS TEQUILA BRAMBLE
PAIRED WITH
PRAWN CEVICHE WITH CROSTINI

THE REFINERY, VANCOUVER, BC
GRAHAM RACICH, MIXOLOGIST
KIRK MORRISON, CHEF

Prepared with a centuries-old method of "cooking" seafood in acidic citric juice instead of heat. Latin-style ceviche is particularly refreshing as a summertime appetizer. The Refinery team balances freshness and acidity by pairing a boldly-flavored ceviche with a botanically inspired, tequila cocktail.

HERBACEOUS TEQUILA BRAMBLE

MAKES 1 SERVING

The history of the Bramble reaches back to Dick Bradsell at Fred's Club in London in the mid-1980s. Originally a gin sour with a float of blackberry syrup, Mr. Racich's version creates a layering effect, a bit of spectacle, as strawberry liqueur slowly winds through the spiked, crushed ice to the bottom of the glass. It's not unlike the feeling of wandering through a wild bramble.

★★★★★

1½ ounces tequila, infused with mint and basil*
1 ounce fresh-squeezed lemon juice
¾ ounce lemon-ginger tea syrup**
½ ounce strawberry liqueur
1 fresh strawberry, for garnish

Fill a collins glass with crushed ice. Add the infused tequila, lemon juice, and lemon-ginger tea syrup. Stir together and top off with more crushed ice. Drizzle the strawberry liqueur over the top and garnish with the fresh strawberry.

*For the tequila infusion: Gently muddle 8 basil leaves and 12 mint leaves in a large glass jar. Add 13 ounces of tequila. Allow to sit for 2 to 4 hours. Strain and refrigerate.

**For the lemon-ginger tea syrup: Add four bar spoons of tea to a container and steep tea for 5 minutes with 1 pint of warm water. Strain steeped tea with a fine mesh strainer, then add the same volume of white granulated sugar to the water (stir to help dissolve). Refrigerate until ready to use.

PRAWN CEVICHE WITH CROSTINI

MAKES 4 TO 6 SERVINGS

Prawns resemble miniature lobsters. "They smell like the sea," says the chef, "and their meat is sweet and succulent." Jalapeño chile provides kick to the prawn ceviche, whose heat and acid are tamed by strawberries and tea syrup in the cocktail.

★ ★ ★ ★ ★

1 pound prawns, peeled and de-veined
1 jalapeño, stem removed, cut into paper-thin rounds
1 shallot, top and bottom removed, halved and cut into thin slices
1 clove of garlic, peeled, cut into thin slices
1 ounce fresh tarragon leaves, stems removed (reserve some for garnishing)
1½ cup white wine vinegar
1½ cup Pharaoh's Heirloom Lemon Vinegar (or freshly pressed lemon juice)
2 cups extra virgin olive oil (plus extra for drizzling)

Using a sharp paring knife, butterfly the prawns by cutting along their backs from head to tail until you have two halves, and place in a plastic bowl. Add the jalapeño, shallot, garlic, and tarragon leaves to the bowl. Season the mixture to taste with sea salt and black pepper. Add the white wine vinegar, heirloom lemon vinegar (or lemon juice), and olive oil, and mix well. Cover with plastic wrap and let marinate in the fridge for a minimum of 3 hours and up to 12 hours.

For the crostini: Preheat oven to 300°F. Thinly slice the baguette on the bias and lay the pieces flat on a baking tray. Drizzle with olive oil and season with salt and pepper. Bake in the oven until crispy and golden brown.

sea salt
black pepper, freshly-ground
1 loaf French baguette

To serve, add an equal portion of ceviche to each of four to six plates, spoon a tablespoon of the marinade over the top. Place a few of the baguette crostinis on the side, and garnish with the extra tarragon leaves.

MEXICAN BRUSH FIRE

PAIRED WITH

OVEN-ROASTED OYSTERS WITH CHILI-TEQUILA BUTTER

B&O AMERICAN BRASSERIE, BALTIMORE, MD
BRENDAN DORR, MIXOLOGIST
THOMAS DUNKLIN, CHEF

Mexico's Santiago de Tequila is the birthplace of the drink that bears its name. Tequila is made from the blue agave plant and harvested from the region's volcanic soils. Mr. Dorr favors artisanal Tanteo tequila with estate-grown jalapeños blended right into the spirit. Jalapeño mingles with the roasted agave base for a dose of savory heat on the finish.

MEXICAN BRUSH FIRE

MAKES 1 SERVING

"It's fun to pair cuisine with spirit origin," says the drinksmith. "Just as I might adapt a sake drink to Japanese cuisine or brandy to a French dish, tequila suits this Mexican-inspired union." Lively fruit components and rich agave of mezcal add a nice complexity to the cocktail while tempering the heat of the infused tequila.

★ ★ ★ ★ ★

1¼ ounce Tanteo Jalapeño Tequila
¼ ounce Los Nahuales Anejo Mezcal
¾ ounce pineapple syrup*
¾ ounce freshly pressed lime juice
1 dash Bittermens Habanero Shrub Bitters
chipotle salt**
coin of fresh jalapeño, for garnish

Combine all liquid ingredients with ice in a shaker. Shake vigorously and strain into a pre-chilled coupe prepared with a chipotle-salted rim.

*In a bowl or 2-quart jar, combine 3 cups of sugar with 3 cups of water and stir. Skin and cube a small pineapple and add the fruit to the sugar mixture. Let stand for 24 hours. Remove the pineapple cubes, lightly pressing them with a hand juicer or using another method to squeeze some juice into the mixture. Stir to dissolve any residual sugar and pour the resulting syrup through a tea strainer or cheesecloth-lined funnel into a 1.5-liter bottle. Add a small dash of vodka as a preservative. Keep refrigerated until ready to use.

**Place ½ cup of kosher salt and ¾ teaspoon of chipotle powder in a small container with a lid, seal the container, and shake vigorously for several seconds until the chipotle powder is evenly distributed in the salt.

OVEN-ROASTED OYSTERS WITH CHILI-TEQUILA BUTTER

MAKES 2 SERVINGS

For James Beard, they were simply "one of the supreme delights that nature has bestowed on man." To the French poet Léon-Paul Fargue, eating oysters was "like kissing the sea on the lips." In this pairing the salty sea taste of oysters is echoed by the chipotle salt on the rim of the drink.

★ ★ ★ ★ ★

For the chili-tequila butter:

½ pound unsalted butter
juice and zest of 1 lime
¼ cup cilantro, minced
1 tablespoon yuzu juice
1 tablespoon tequila
1 Serrano chili, minced
1 tablespoon extra virgin olive oil
salt and black pepper, to taste

For the dish:

12 oysters, fresh in the shell
chili-tequila butter (from above)

Soften the unsalted butter. Combine ingredients and blend in a food processor. Wrap the mixture in plastic wrap, roll into a log, and chill in the fridge to stiffen.

Preheat oven to 450°F. Remove top shell of oysters; loosen meat. Arrange in half-shells on baking sheet. Slice the chilled butter into coins (about 1 tablespoon size) and place one on top of each oyster. Bake oysters 3 to 4 minutes. Remove from the oven and serve immediately. Make sure to have plenty of crusty bread on hand for mopping up the butter and oyster juices left on the serving platter.

JUNIPER'S TWIST

PAIRED WITH

ESCOLAR-STUFFED WHITE MUSHROOMS

MOSHI MOSHI SUSHI, SEATTLE, WA
JEANNINE KAPTEYN, MIXOLOGIST
CHONG KIM, CHEF

Japanese food is prepared with care, with special attention to balancing flavors. The cocktail in this sushi bar pairing features gin, whose botanicals come to life in the cocktail and complement the dish without masking its flavors.

Juniper's Twist and Escolar-Stuffed White Mushrooms

JUNIPER'S TWIST

MAKES 1 SERVING

"This drink has many layers," explains Ms. Kapteyn. "Gin is the main spirit, supporting (in combination with Genever) the cocktail with delicate resinous notes of juniper, while the Nonino connects to the earthiness of the mushrooms, and the elderflower adds both subtle sweetness and floral nose."

★ ★ ★ ★ ★

1½ ounce London Dry Gin
½ ounce Amara Nonino
½ ounce Pür Spirits Elderflower
¼ ounce Bols Genever
1 dash orange bitters
orange peel twist

Combine all liquid ingredients into a mixing glass filled with ice. Stir to chill and strain into a pre-chilled coupe. Squeeze the orange peel over the surface to express the oil and drop into the cocktail.

ESCOLAR-STUFFED WHITE MUSHROOMS

MAKES 4 SERVINGS

The firm flesh and rich flavor of escolar is a revelation in Chef Kim's Korean-inspired dish that practically melts in your mouth. "The cocktail's subtle zesty-orange component boosts the ponzu's tart, citrus notes to complement the raw fish, while the liqueurs harmonize with buttery and earthy elements of the dish."

★ ★ ★ ★ ★

12 small white mushrooms
¼ cup red onions, chopped
1 ½ ounces escolar (or salmon), sashimi grade
2 tablespoons ponzu (citrus soy sauce)
2 tablespoons olive oil
1 tablespoon sliced green onions or chives
salt and pepper, to taste

Dice escolar into ⅛-inch cubes. Remove stems from caps of mushrooms. Clean mushroom caps by peeling off outer layer of skin. Over medium heat pour olive oil in sauté pan, warm, and add mushroom caps bottoms down, cover with lid, and cook about 3 minutes. Reduce heat to low and cook for another 3 minutes. Remove mushrooms from pan. Add chopped red onions (about ¼ teaspoon per mushroom). Add chopped escolar to fill/top mushroom (1 teaspoon per mushroom). Season with salt and pepper. Lightly cover each mushroom with ponzu. Sprinkle green onions over the top of each.

THE LAST WORD

PAIRED WITH

"STILL LIFE" WITH GARDEN TOMATOES, RICOTTA, CRISPY CHICKEN SKIN, AND BASIL

THE DELMONICO ROOM (AT THE HOTEL FAUCHÈRE), MILFORD, PA
CHRISTOPHER BATES, CHEF AND BEVERAGE MANAGER

This chef-crafted pairing employs a gin-based, Prohibition-era cocktail to elevate an artfully composed salad to its rightful place. "When serving cocktails with food, you take into account the flavor profile of each ingredient," explains Mr. Bates, whose wine background aids him in creating his cocktail pairings.

THE LAST WORD

MAKES 1 SERVING

Browsing through a copy of Ted Saucier's *Bottoms Up!* (1951), Chef Bates decided to dust off this nearly-forgotten, easy to assemble palate cleanser. It's a perfectly balanced sipper: a little sour, a little sweet, a little pungent. "I suspect this cocktail is called 'The Last Word' because it lingers after you're done," he explains. "It leaves an aftertaste of herbs, licorice, citrus, cherries, and juniper—lovely partners with the salad."

★ ★ ★ ★ ★

¼ ounce gin
¾ ounce Maraschino liquor (Luxardo)
¾ ounce Green Chartreuse
¾ ounce freshly pressed lime juice

Combine all ingredients in a mixing glass filled with ice. Shake vigorously and double strain into a pre-chilled cocktail glass. Serve without garnish.

"STILL LIFE" WITH GARDEN TOMATOES, RICOTTA, CRISPY CHICKEN SKIN, AND BASIL

MAKES 4 SERVINGS

Herbaceous, naturally Green Chartreuse, is made from herbs, plants, and flowers, macerated in alcohol, and steeped for about 8 hours. In this French-inspired *salade composée*, basil seeds are hydrated in the liqueur, providing a subtle bridge to the cocktail. "Use as many varieties of heirloom tomatoes as you can find," suggests the chef, "with at least three colors."

★ ★ ★ ★ ★

For the ricotta mix:

1 cup high-quality ricotta cheese
2 tablespoons extra virgin olive oil
salt and pepper, to taste

Wisk together and put in piping bag with a half-inch tip.

For the pesto:

2 cups basil leaves (or other green herb), packed
⅓ cup walnuts, toasted
3 garlic cloves, minced
½ cup pecorino romano cheese, shredded
½ cup extra-virgin olive oil
salt and pepper, to taste

Blend in food processor until smooth, put in a jar, and cover with more olive oil.

For the basil seeds:

4 tablespoons basil seeds
½ cup warm water
2 tablespoons Green Chartreuse

Soak seeds for ½ hour with water and Chartreuse.

For the chicken skins:

3 chicken skins
salt and pepper

Preheat oven to 350°F. Line a baking tray with parchment paper or aluminum foil. Lay skins flat and season with salt and pepper. Bake until golden and crunchy, about 10 minutes.

For the plates:

4 large or 6 medium heirloom tomatoes, mixed varieties
basil leaves and edible flowers
Sel Gris (French grey sea salt) or Maldon sea salt
black pepper, freshly cracked
extra virgin olive oil

Pipe a squiggly line of ricotta onto each of four serving plates (be artful). Cut each tomato in different ways (depending on size and shape, but try to keep integrity of the tomato). Place tomatoes on ricotta, pushing them in to hold them in place. Scatter basil leaves and flowers throughout tomatoes. Spoon over the pesto (loosen with olive oil as needed). Spoon drops of the hydrated basil seeds over the top. Break chicken skin into small pieces and stand pieces throughout the tomatoes. Sprinkle with salt and pepper and drizzle with the olive oil.

BETTER LIVING

PAIRED WITH

CUCUMBER SALAD WITH STRAWBERRIES AND GRILLED RICOTTA SALATA

BOKA RESTAURANT + BAR, CHICAGO, IL
BENJAMIN SCHILLER, MIXOLOGIST
CARL SHELTON, CHEF

Noting that Thai cuisine adds sliced cucumbers as crisp, refreshing sides to many of its dishes, Mr. Shelton's cucumber-centered medley becomes a boon companion to Mr. Schiller's Thai-inspired cocktail. With an orchestra of flavors that hits all the notes—sweet, savory, spicy, bitter, salty, and acidic—cocktail and dish are perfectly balanced.

BETTER LIVING

MAKES 1 SERVING

The drink corrals a mélange of influences, combining rum with aquavit and ginger along with lime juice and bitters that add a kick to the mix (even though they are only used in dashes). It's a suave composite with many flavor nuances common to Thai cuisine.

★ ★ ★ ★ ★

1½ ounces aquavit
½ ounce rum
¾ ounce ginger syrup*
¾ ounce fresh-squeezed lime juice
3 dashes Reagan's Orange Bitters
2 dashes Angostura Bitters (Float)
soda water

Combine aquavit, rum, ginger syrup, lime juice, and orange bitters in a shaker. Add ice, shake, and strain into collins glass filled with ice. Top with soda and float 2 dashes of Angostura Bitters.

*For the ginger syrup: Peel 2 pounds of ginger root, and then juice. Strain through a chinois and measure yield. Transfer juice to pan and add an equal amount of sugar. Bring mixture to a boil, transfer to an ice bath, and then bottle.

CUCUMBER SALAD WITH STRAWBERRIES AND GRILLED RICOTTA SALATA

MAKES 6 SERVINGS

Select firm, unblemished cukes, dark green and rounded at the tips. They take center stage in a crisp, refreshing accompaniment to Mr. Schiller's cocktail. Fragrant Thai basil and minty-fennely shiso leaves bring distinctive flavors to the dish. A thin slice of ricotta salada on top adds salt and depth to a salad that is as fun to look at as it is to eat.

★ ★ ★ ★ ★

6 cups cucumbers, peeled, quartered lengthwise (seeds removed), and cut into triangles
3 cups sliced strawberries
3 tablespoons extra virgin olive oil
3 cups pickled, sliced green strawberries*
2 tablespoons Thai basil, chiffonade
2 tablespoons shiso leaves, chiffonade
½ cup ricotta salada, grilled and sliced**
kosher salt

Toss olive oil and cucumbers in a bowl and season with salt and pepper. Add pickled strawberries, sliced strawberries, and shiso. Place in a serving bowl and top with ricotta salada.

*For the pickled green strawberries:

3 cups green strawberries
2½ cups white balsamic vinegar
1½ cups Lillet Rouge
½ cup honey
2 tablespoons ginger, chopped
1 jalapeno, seeded-veined, chopped
1 stalk lemongrass
2 tablespoons coriander, toasted
1 teaspoon clove, toasted
2 tablespoons juniper, toasted
2 tablespoons allspice, toasted

Clean strawberries and cut off greens. Heat vinegar, Lillet, honey, and spices until they reach a boil. Turn off heat and pour over green strawberries in a metal pan. Let strawberries naturally come down to room temperature, slice, and store in pickling liquid.

**For the grilled ricotta salada:

½ cup ricotta salada
1 tablespoon vegetable oil

Slice ricotta salada into ¼-inch thick pieces. Brush lightly with vegetable oil and grill just enough to get cross hatches.

SAVANNAH SPOKEN WORD

PAIRED WITH

SNAPPER CRUDO WITH JUNIPER-INFUSED BUTTER

LOCAL 11 TEN, SAVANNAH, GA
RYAN HALL, MIXOLOGIST
JACOB HAMMER, CHEF

While there are more than one hundred botanical ingredients used in the production of gin, the distinctive piney flavor comes from small, round, bluish-black berries—not true berries at all, but scales on the cones of prickly juniper bushes. As Mr. Hall and Mr. Hammer conduct their respective arias, herbs play assertive roles in harmonizing cocktail and dish. It's a pairing in the key of juniper.

SAVANNAH SPOKEN WORD

Mr. Hall borrows the name of his drink from the city's festival of poetry slams, so it's not surprising that he takes poetic license with the Prohibition-era Last Word cocktail. His rendition revs up the proportion of a botanically-rich gin and adds a dash of orange bitters.

★ ★ ★ ★ ★

1½ ounces Uncle Val's Botanical Gin
1 ounce Green Chartreuse
½ ounce freshly pressed lime juice
1 ounce maraschino liqueur
1 dash orange bitters

Combine all ingredients in a mixing glass filled with ice. Shake vigorously and double strain into a pre-chilled cocktail glass. Serve without garnish.

SNAPPER CRUDO WITH JUNIPER-INFUSED BUTTER

MAKES 4 SERVINGS

The crudo is unexpectedly lively, silky, and intense. Tarragon imparts its flavor readily in the drizzle of gastrique, and the last-minute swirl of warm herbal butter invades the palate, kissing the lips at each encounter and releasing a perfume of juniper to mirror the cocktail. The success of crudo depends on the quality of the seafood used, so buy only fresh sashimi-grade red snapper.

★ ★ ★ ★ ★

For the juniper-infused butter:

1 pound butter
2 bay leaves
5 dry juniper berries
1 orange peel

In a small sauce pot, combine butter, bay leaves, juniper berries, and orange peel. Place on medium-low heat. When butter begins to separate, solids from fat, skim solids from the top. The infused butter is finished when it is free of milk fats and completely clarified. Do not allow it to turn brown or begin to burn. Strain into another sauce pot for later heating.

For the tarragon gastrique:

½ cup granulated sugar
2 cups honey
1 pint champagne vinegar
1 tablespoon fresh tarragon

In a medium sauce pot, combine sugar, honey, and champagne vinegar. Place mixture on medium heat and bring to a simmer. Continue at a simmer, not a boil, until it reduces by about one-third. Add the tarragon and reduce until the sauce thickens enough to coat the back of a spoon. Strain and reserve.

For the dish:

*1 red snapper fillet, extremely fresh,
cleaned
6 baby lemon sorrel leaves
3 kaffir lime leaves
2 small spicy peppers, cayenne, thinly
sliced
tarragon gastrique (from above)
juniper-infused butter (from above)
1 ounce Maldon finishing salt*

Slice the filet on a bias, very thin. Arrange sliced fish, as desired, on a plate, cover with plastic wrap, and refrigerate until ready to use. To finish dish, heat the infused butter to 115°F. Unwrap snapper and garnish the plate with sorrel, lime leaves, and sliced peppers. Drizzle dish with 1 tablespoon of the gastrique, then drizzle with 1 tablespoon of the infused butter. Sprinkle with a pinch of the salt.

THE WHISKEY SHIVER

PAIRED WITH

ROASTED SWEET POTATOES

WITH GREMOLATA AND PEPPER JAM

MERCHANT, MADISON, WI
TOM DUFEK, MIXOLOGIST
ANNA DICKSON, CHEF

Keeping faith with a colonial-era method of preserving fruits for the off-season, Mr. Dufek turns plums, vinegar, and a sweetener into an intensely-flavored "shrub," a concentrate of fruit essence that lends a tangy edge to his cocktail. "We applied this historical trick of the trade to plums and captured a taste of fall in a mix with bourbon, smoke, and warm spices," he explains. "It just begs for the pairing with savory sweet potatoes."

THE WHISKEY SHIVER

MAKES 1 SERVING

Subversion is afoot in what starts out as a Bourbon Sour and then becomes something of an amalgam. Sweet, sour, and fruity, the shrub simultaneously quenches thirst and whets the appetite for the hearty dish. The characteristic sweetness of bourbon softens the sharpness of vinegar, as the tobacco's woodsy richness marries with the darker qualities of the fruit—in all, a comforting set of flavors.

★ ★ ★ ★ ★

For the plum shrub:

½ pound ripe plums, peeled, pitted, and cubed
½ pound brown sugar
white balsamic vinegar

Toss plums in the sugar, ensuring plums are completely covered by sugar and all sugar is incorporated. Let rest in refrigerator for 24 hours. Stir and incorporate any sugar that has sunk to the bottom. Let rest in refrigerator for an additional 24 hours. Strain plums from liquid, squeezing gently. Measure liquid and add 1 part white balsamic vinegar for every 10 parts liquid and stir to incorporate. Return to refrigerator until ready to use.

For the tobacco tincture:

½ cup high-proof rum
3 cinnamon sticks, roughly broken
25 allspice berries, roughly crushed
1 ounce loose leaf pipe tobacco

Add all ingredients and let rest for 48 hours in a dark place. Strain out solids through a cheese cloth. Set aside until ready to use.

For the drink:

Isle Scotch, for rinse
1¾ ounces bourbon
¾ ounce freshly pressed lemon juice
¾ ounce plum shrub (from above)
2 dashes Angostura bitters
15 drops spiced tobacco tincture (from above)
freshly-grated cinnamon

Pour a small amount of the scotch into a pre-chilled cocktail glass and rotate to coat the inner surface. Combine bourbon, lemon juice, shrub, bitters, and tobacco tincture with ice in a shaker. Shake vigorously and double strain into the prepared glass. Dust the top with cinnamon.

ROASTED SWEET POTATOES
WITH GREMOLATA AND PEPPER JAM

MAKES 6 TO 8 SERVINGS

Roasting sweet potatoes slightly concentrates their natural sweetness. "Brown sugar and spice in the sweet pepper jam excites other flavors in both cocktail and dish," says Ms. Dickson, "reinforcing the pairing concept." Thankfully, the delightful complexity of the cocktail fits in with the ingredients of the dish like pieces of a mosaic. No duplication. Just balance and harmony.

★ ★ ★ ★ ★

For the gremolata:

1 head garlic, peeled and minced
1 bunch parsley, minced
zest and juice of 5 lemons
4 tablespoons olive oil

Thoroughly combine all ingredients in a small bowl, cover with plastic, and refrigerate until ready to use.

For the pepper jam:

2 cups piquillo peppers, roasted and peeled
3 tablespoons tomato paste
3 tablespoons brown sugar
1 tablespoon honey
1 teaspoon salt
½ teaspoon black pepper, freshly cracked

Combine all ingredients in a sauté pan over medium heat and bring to a simmer. Remove from heat and allow to cool.

For the dish:

4 large sweet potatoes
1 teaspoon salt
canola oil, for frying
gremolata (from above)
pepper jam (from above)

Peel and dice sweet potatoes into 1-inch sticks (cut on bias). Blanch potatoes for 3 minutes. Bake for 30 minutes at 300°F, then deep fry at 375°F until golden brown, about 5 minutes. Season with salt, and toss with the gremolata while warm. Serve with the pepper jam.

THE SUNDAY MORNING

PAIRED WITH

BLUE CORN HUSHPUPPIES

WITH VOODOO DIPPING SAUCE

CHURCH BAR, PORTLAND, OR
CHRISTOPHER COOK, MIXOLOGIST
JAVIER CHIN, CHEF

We're reminded of F. Scott Fitzgerald's words in *May Day*: "It was impossible for their joint imaginations to conjure up a world where anyone might object to anyone else having champagne for breakfast." It's an idea wholeheartedly embraced for a Southern Sunday, brunch-inspired pairing of a bubbly cocktail with crispy hushpuppies, kicked up with a peppery dipping sauce.

THE SUNDAY MORNING

The drinksmith's brunch-appropriate champagne cocktail displays a range of influences—oak of bourbon, and tang of ginger mixed with citrus and bitters. Sparkling bubbles propel essences to the top of the drink, magnifying flavors. To further quote Mr. Fitzgerald, "Here's to alcohol, the rose-colored glasses of life."

★ ★ ★ ★ ★

1 ounce Buffalo Trace Bourbon
½ ounce ginger syrup
½ ounce freshly pressed lemon juice
3 dashes Angostura bitters
champagne, to top up

Combine bourbon, ginger syrup, lemon juice, and bitters with ice in a shaker. Shake vigorously and double strain into a pre-chilled champagne flute. Top up with champagne.

BLUE CORN HUSHPUPPIES
WITH VOODOO DIPPING SAUCE

MAKES 16 TO 20 HUSHPUPPIES

Legend has it that Southern fishermen and hunters first made the golden nuggets from scraps to quiet barking dogs with the command, "Hush, puppy." Deep-fried, finger-shaped dumplings of cornmeal live on in Southern cuisine as staples of a proper New Orleans brunch. Mr. Chin connects savory hushpuppies to the fizzy cocktail with a Creole-style dipping sauce flavored with lemon and ginger.

★ ★ ★ ★ ★

For the voodoo sauce:

½ tablespoon crushed red pepper
1 tablespoon fresh ginger, grated
3 cups vegetable stock
1 cup granulated sugar
1 tablespoon freshly pressed lemon juice

Combine ingredients in small stockpot. Cook over medium heat 30 minutes, stirring gently often. Reduce down until it becomes a syrup. Remove from heat and set aside to cool. Mixture will be thick and fragrant.

For the hushpuppies:

3 cups all-purpose flour
½ cup blue corn meal
1 tablespoon baking powder
½ tablespoon sugar
½ tablespoon black pepper
½ tablespoon salt
¾ tablespoon baking soda
½ teaspoon cayenne powder
3 eggs, slightly beaten
1¾ cups buttermilk
¾ cups chopped green onions
1½ cups whole corn kernels
4 cups canola oil, for frying

Combine dry ingredients in a large mixing bowl. In a separate bowl, combine beaten eggs, buttermilk, green onions, and corn. Whisk wet ingredients into dry ingredients. Using a deep pot, preheat oil for frying to 350°F. Drop the batter, 1 teaspoon at a time, into the oil. (Dip the spoon in a glass of water after each hushpuppy is dropped in the oil). Fry until golden brown, turning the hushpuppies during cooking.

RIGHT UP MY ALLEY

PAIRED WITH

LAMB TARTARE WITH CELERY ROOT REMOULADE

LONGMAN & EAGLE, CHICAGO, IL
DEREK ALEXANDER, MIXOLOGIST
JARED WENTWORTH, CHEF

The notion that a proper Manhattan Cocktail should be made with rye has taken hold in many quarters, including this Chicago destination for classics-with-a-twist. After all, the spicier profile of rye balances so well with sweet vermouth and bitters. The cocktail and dish selected for this pairing may seem familiar, but the recipes are decidedly not.

RIGHT UP MY ALLEY

MAKES 1 SERVING

It is said that a Manhattan loses much of its soul without bitters. In his homage to the Manhattan, Mr. Alexander ramps up bitter influence on the complex, earthy spice of rye with layers of herbal bitterness from both Cynar and Bonal Gentiane Quina, complicated with capricious notes of artichokes, honey, and plums.

★ ★ ★ ★ ★

2 ounces Rittenhouse Rye (100 Proof)
½ ounce Cynar
½ ounces Bonal Gentiane Quina
½ ounces Carpani Antica vermouth
3 dashes Peychaud's Bitters

Combine all ingredients with ice in a mixing glass. Stir to chill and strain into a pre-chilled Old Fashioned glass. Serve without garnish.

LAMB TARTARE WITH CELERY ROOT REMOULADE

MAKES 4 SERVINGS

For the tartare, Chef Wentworth goes off-script, using lamb loin instead of traditional beef, hand-cutting for best texture. He combines classic additions, like anchovies and capers, with unconventional ones, like black olives and fresh rosemary. Bold and complex, the accompanying cocktail offers just enough flavor and alcohol to balance this powerfully built dish.

★ ★ ★ ★ ★

For the remoulade:

1 celery root
½ ounce chopped parsley
½ ounce chopped capers
2 tablespoons whole grain mustard
salt and pepper, to taste

Peel the root and cut into large dice. Boil until soft, and then purée in food processor with the parsley, caper, and all the whole grain mustard. Season with salt and pepper and reserve.

For the dish:

8 ounces hand-diced lamb loin
4 quail egg yolks
1 tablespoon Dijon mustard
½ ounce chopped parsley
½ ounce chopped capers
2 slices stale pumpernickel bread
3 Spanish anchovies, chopped fine
1 teaspoon freshly chopped rosemary
¼ cup pitted black olives, julienned
¼ cup extra virgin oil
remoulade (from above)
Perigord black truffle, for garnish

Place diced lamb in a mixing bowl. Mix with 4 quail egg yolks, Dijon, caper, and parsley, mix well, and reserve. Put dried pumpernickel in coffee grinder and buzz till a powder forms. Mix anchovies, rosemary, and black olives with olive oil. Portion remoulade in the middle of four plates. Top each with a quenelle (football-shaped scoop) of tartare. Spoon anchovy-olive mixture around each plate, dust with pumpernickel "powder," and garnish with shaved black truffle.

Sweet Onion Soup with Bone Marrow Dumplings

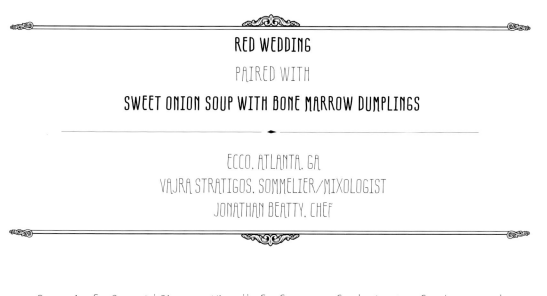

RED WEDDING

PAIRED WITH

SWEET ONION SOUP WITH BONE MARROW DUMPLINGS

ECCO, ATLANTA, GA
VAJRA STRATIGOS, SOMMELIER/MIXOLOGIST
JONATHAN BEATTY, CHEF

One recipe for Soupe à l'Oignon au Vin calls for four cups of red wine (one for the soup and three to drink while cooking). A good, dry, hearty red wine is the common ingredient in Chef Beatty's elevated version of french onion soup and the attendant cocktail. Mr. Stratigos explains, "Rich beef broth, stews, and alike savory, concentrated preparations in French cookery are often well suited to a vinous counterpoint as a beverage pairing."

RED WEDDING

MAKES 1 SERVING

"The chef and I both felt that incorporating the virtues of a wine as fortification to a spirit would result in a similar balancing act as one might find with a wine and soup alone," says Mr. Stratigos. "The exotic aroma and increased alcohol in the cocktail make for a singular expression that suits the preparation."

★ ★ ★ ★ ★

1 ounce Olivares Dulce Monastrell or other hearty red wine
1 ounce Dolin Rouge or other sweet vermouth
½ ounce Fidencio Mezcal Clasico or other mezcal
spritz Fernet Branca
lemon peel medallion

Combine the wine, vermouth, and mezcal in a mixing glass filled with ice. Stir to chill and strain into a martini glass. Spritz with Fernet Branca. Squeeze lemon peel over the surface to express oils and drop into the cocktail.

Red Wedding

SWEET ONION SOUP WITH BONE MARROW DUMPLINGS

MAKES 4 TO 6 SERVINGS

"Bone marrow is an often misunderstood piece of culinary lore," insists Chef Beatty. "When you use bone marrow in an application with a beefy flavor, it's like putting the flavor profile on steroids. In this dish I use the marrow in pillowy dumplings—with each bite you experience the rich unctuousness of bone marrow set against the sweet onions and light acidity from the red wine-enriched beef stock." There is both a physical and chemical balancing that takes place in this pairing—the wine's structure and tannic components work in tandem with the distillate to drive the flavors of the soup and clean and prepare the palate for the next spoonful.

★ ★ ★ ★ ★

For the dumplings:

1 ½ cups bone marrow
1 cup flour
1 teaspoon baking powder
1 ½ cups fine breadcrumbs
2 eggs
salt and pepper, to taste

Chop the raw bone marrow and mix with flour, baking powder, bread crumbs, egg, salt, and pepper. Form dumplings into small golf balls and poach in onion soup for 4 to 5 minutes until they float to the surface. Set aside.

For the soup:

¼ cup butter
8 Spanish or sweet onions, thinly sliced
kosher salt
black pepper, freshly cracked
1 cup red wine
½ cup sherry
6 cups veal (or beef) stock
red wine vinegar, if needed
⅔ pound Gruyère or Emmanthaler cheese, grated
dumplings (from above)

Using a pot large enough to hold all the onions, place the pot over medium heat, and melt the butter. Add the onions, sprinkle with 2 teaspoons salt, cover, and cook until the onions have heated through and started to steam. Uncover, reduce the heat to low, and cook, stirring occasionally, until the onions have completely cooked down, the water has cooked off, and the onions have turned a dark amber color, roughly 3 to 4 hours. Season with several grinds of pepper. Deglaze with red wine and reduce to *au sec* (nearly dry). Add in 6 cups veal stock. Raise the heat to high and bring the soup to a simmer, then reduce the heat to low. Add the sherry. Taste and season with salt and pepper as needed. If the soup is too sweet, add some red wine vinegar. Adjust seasoning with salt and pepper. Preheat the broiler/grill. Portion the soup into bowls, float the dumplings on top, cover with the cheese, and broil/grill until the cheese is melted and nicely browned. Serve immediately.

SAZERAC

PAIRED WITH

CALF SWEETBREADS WITH DUMPLINGS

PÉCHÉ, AUSTIN, TX
ROB PATE, BARTENDER
JASON DODGE, CHEF

Péché means "sin," explains Rob Pate, whose fondness for absinthe, the once-banned spirit, and classic European-style cookery defines his establishment. Dear to his cocktail geek's heart, absinthe provides anise-flavored coating to the glass of a properly-made Sazerac in a pairing with the richness and decadent flavor of sweetbreads and buttery dumplings. The strong cocktail becomes a foil whose character emphasizes the strengths of the dish.

SAZERAC

MAKES 1 SERVING

It's a complex, spirit-forward drink that requires attention to detail, proper technique, and the right proportions to fully reveal its brilliance. Floral aromatics of the Peychaud's gentian-based bitters open up flavors of the rye, and the expression of lemon oils provide light and spark to the cocktail.

★★★★★

3 ounces rye whiskey
¾ ounce simple syrup
Peychaud bitters, to taste
absinthe
lemon twist

Chill an Old Fashioned glass by filling it with ice and letting it sit while preparing the rest of the drink. In a separate mixing glass, muddle the simple syrup and Peychaud bitters together. Add the rye whiskey and ice to the bitters mixture and stir gently. Discard the ice in the chilled glass and rinse it with absinthe by pouring a small amount into the glass, swirling it around and discarding the liquid. Strain the whiskey mixture from the mixing glass into the Old Fashioned glass. Lemon twist should be squeezed over the drink to release its essences, but the twist should not be dropped into the glass itself.

CALF SWEETBREADS WITH DUMPLINGS

MAKES 4 TO 6 SERVINGS

Sweetbreads are the thymus, a gland located in a young calf's chest and throat area that diminish in size as the animal matures. The smoothly bitter and spicy notes of the Sazerac help take the edge off the creamy, tender glands. "With such a full-flavored entrée," explains the chef, "you need a just-as-strong drink to balance it. This pairing is not for the weak-hearted."

★ ★ ★ ★ ★

For the dumplings:

1 cup all-purpose flour
2 teaspoons baking powder
½ teaspoon salt
1 tablespoon fresh chopped parsley, optional
1 tablespoon butter
⅓ to ½ cup milk

Combine the flour, baking powder, and salt in a medium bowl. Cut in the butter until blended. Stir in milk to form a wet dough. (It should be thin enough to drop from a wet spoon). When sweetbreads stock is simmering, put spoonfuls of the batter in the stock, trying not to submerge them in the liquid but let them be held up by meat and/or vegetables. Cook, uncovered, for 10 minutes. Cover tightly and cook 10 minutes longer. Makes about 8 dumplings, depending on size.

For the dish:

4 (9-ounce) pieces calf sweetbreads,
halved
milk, enough to cover
salt
juice of half a lemon
¼ cup canola oil
8 tablespoons butter
black pepper, freshly cracked
¼ cup Noilly Prat dry vermouth
1 cup beef stock
¼ pound haricots verts, trimmed and
steamed
16 pearl onions, peeled and boiled
¼ pound baby carrots, peeled,
trimmed, and steamed
dumplings (from above)
2 tablespoons minced flat-leaf
parsley, for garnish

Wash sweetbreads in cold water, then put them in a large bowl, cover with ice water and milk, and refrigerate overnight.

Discard milk/water, rinse well, and drain. Put sweetbreads in a saucepan, cover with cold salted water, add lemon juice, and bring to a boil over medium heat. Boil for 1 minute. Drain, then transfer to a bowl of ice water to cool them. When cool, clean by removing and discarding all fat and sinew. Blot dry with a kitchen towel, wrap in plastic, and refrigerate overnight.

Preheat oven to 325°F. Heat oil and 4 tablespoons butter in a large ovenproof skillet over medium heat until butter begins to sizzle. Generously season sweetbreads with salt and pepper, then sauté until just browned, about 5 minutes per side. Add 3 tablespoons butter and transfer skillet to oven for 20 minutes. Remove skillet from oven, transfer sweetbreads to a platter and keep warm. Pour off fat, place skillet over medium heat, add vermouth, and cook for 1 minute, stirring with a wooden spoon to loosen any brown bits (fond) stuck to the bottom of the pan. Add stock and reduce by half. Melt remaining 1 tablespoon butter in a large sauté pan over medium heat, pour in ¼ cup of sauce, then add haricots verts, onions, and carrots. Season to taste with salt and pepper. Add dumplings and cook until vegetables and dumplings are heated through. Arrange vegetables and dumplings around sweetbreads on the platter. Spoon remaining sauce over sweetbreads and dumplings, then sprinkle with parsley.

CANE SALATO

PAIRED WITH

GRILLED ESCAROLE "SOTTO ACETI"

LEGUME BISTRO/BUTTERJOINT, PITTSBURGH, PA
WILL GROVES, MIXOLOGIST
TREVETT HOOPER, CHEF

"Our goal is to create experiences that are predictably inspired and expressive of the place we live at this moment in time," explains Chef Hooper, whose collaboration with bar manager Will Groves offers a delightful aperitif/antipasto alliance. The viscosity and citric character of the cocktail cut the fattiness of the bacon and complement the acidity of the pickled vegetables.

CANE SALATO

MAKES 1 SERVING

Cane salato is Italian for "salty dog," and according to Mr. Groves, his drink is an Italian-influenced riff on a Salty Dog (the classic vodka-grapefruit cocktail served in a glass with a salted rim). The pinch of salt added to the low-alcohol drink rounds off some of its leafy bitterness, while the vermouth adds rich, layered, companionable flavors to the pairing.

★ ★ ★ ★ ★

1 ½ ounces Carpano Antica Formula sweet vermouth
1 ounce fresh-squeezed grapefruit juice
1 pinch kosher salt
2 ounces dry sparkling wine, such as Prosecco
Grapefruit peel, for garnish

Add vermouth, grapefruit juice, and salt to a mixing glass. Stir briefly without ice to dissolve salt. Add ice and stir to chill. Strain into a pre-chilled cocktail glass. Top off with sparkling wine and garnish with a strip of grapefruit peel.

GRILLED ESCAROLE "SOTTO ACETI"

MAKES 4 SERVINGS

Italian giardiniera, also called "sotto aceti" (or "under vinegar"), is an array of vegetables (usually, carrots, red pepper, celery, and cauliflower), preserved to maintain their distinctive flavors and textures. The sub-acid of the cocktail's grapefruit component finds harmony with the complex flavors and textures of the mix.

★ ★ ★ ★ ★

For the mustard vinaigrette:

1 clove garlic
2 tablespoons sherry vinegar
¼ cup red wine vinegar
3 tablespoons Dijon mustard
1⅓ cup extra virgin olive oil

For the salad:

2 heads escarole
olive oil
salt and pepper
½ cup giardiniera (traditional or spicy)
8 strips bacon, cooked crispy
mustard vinaigrette (from above)
parmesan cheese

Pulverize garlic with a little salt in a mortar and pestle, or lacking that, just chop the garlic and salt together on the cutting board until it almost liquefies. In a bowl, whisk together the garlic, vinegars, and mustard. Slowly drizzle in the oil. Season to taste with salt and pepper.

Cut the escarole in half lengthwise, so that the leaves stay attached to the core at the bottom. Trim off any dark green outer leaves, so that what you end up with is a bundle of the heartier, light green–colored inner leaves. Let soak for a few minutes in water, to loosen up any dirt that may be in the head. Shake the trimmed, halved heads vigorously until they are pretty dry. Pat dry with paper towels. Toss the escarole halves with a little olive oil and salt and pepper. Grill over a hot grill for one minute on one side, or until some of the leaves begin to char. Flip over and cook until warmed through. Plate, and portion with the giardiniera and bacon. Drizzle vinaigrette over the top, then finish with freshly-shaved parmesan.

DISCO VOLANTE

PAIRED WITH

THAI-STYLE CHICKEN WINGS

CHANTANEE THAI RESTAURANT AND BAR, BELLEVUE, WA
JASON SAURA, MIXOLOGIST
SUPAT WARAPATTARADILOK, CHEF

Bangkok meets Buffalo—a confluence of spices and herbs used in Thai cooking becomes increasingly bold, rich, and spicy with each bite and, like its American counterpart, builds on the palate like a gastronomical crescendo. Although flavor combinations are studies in contrast, the pairing balances a big, rich dish with an equally big, bold cocktail. Neither is intimidated by the other.

DISCO VOLANTE

MAKES 1 SERVING

The Disco Volante (Italian for "flying saucer") is named after the hydrofoil craft owned by SPECTRE agent Emilio Largo in *Thunderball*, the James Bond novel and film. The dramatic composition of twenty-three-year-old Guatemalan rum, combined with pungent Fernet Branca, tangy ginger, and creamy whole egg, with a dash of bitters and a grind of fresh nutmeg, has the depth and power to stand up to the fiery wings.

★ ★ ★ ★ ★

1 ounce aged rum (such as Ron Zacapa 23)
¾ ounce Fernet Branca
¾ ounce ginger syrup
1 whole egg
2 to 3 dashes Angostura bitters
fresh-grated nutmeg

Add rum, Fernet, ginger syrup, and whole egg to a shaker and dry-shake (shake without ice). Add ice and shake again until well chilled. Strain into pre-chilled cocktail glass. Dash with bitters and lightly dust with nutmeg.

THAI-STYLE CHICKEN WINGS

MAKES 4 TO 6 SERVINGS

If there's a downside in a pairing of this scope, it's focusing on any one ingredient. While Thai chili peppers steal the thunder with heat and aromatics, other ingredients add depth and complexity. Salty oyster sauce gives tone, garlic lends a pungent accent, and soy sauce adds savor.

★ ★ ★ ★ ★

12 pieces chicken wings
12 medium Thai basil leaves, finely chopped
2 tablespoons vegetable oil, plus more for frying
2 tablespoons oyster sauce
1 tablespoon finely chopped bell pepper
1 teaspoon finely chopped Thai chili pepper
1 teaspoon sugar
1 teaspoon soy sauce
1 teaspoon minced garlic

Heat oil in deep fryer or high-walled skillet (about 1½ inches deep) on high heat. Add wings and cook until brown and crisp, then let the oil drain on a cooling rack. Prepare the sauce by adding the remainder of ingredients to a skillet or wok. Cook on high heat until slightly thickened. Add the wings to the skillet/wok to reheat and cover with sauce. Remove from heat. Place wings on a plate and drizzle the extra sauce over the top.

NIGHTSHADE

PAIRED WITH

ESCABECHE DE PESCADO IN AVOCADO CUPS

GEORGE'S AT THE COVE, LA JOLLA, CA
FRANKIE THAHELD, MIXOLOGIST
TREY FOSHEE, CHEF

The ingredient-driven pairing is fostered by the *terroir*, or "sense of place," of the California Coast. "With cocktails, it is important to think smaller portions for smaller dishes," explains Mr. Thaheld. "These are often richer, more flavorful (and concentrated) foods, and cocktail flavors can be more concentrated and fine-tuned to an individual dish. The relationship creates a closed loop between kitchen and bar, assuring a more complete dining experience."

NIGHTSHADE

Embracing a philosophy one might call "farm-to-bar," the drinksmith calls on fresh local produce to play as important a role as the spirit. A species of nightshade plants, tomatoes lend their own natural balance between sweetness and acidity to a blend with grassy onions, unfiltered vodka, sugar, and citrus—a composition that pairs brilliantly with the dish.

★ ★ ★ ★ ★

¼ yellow tomato
1 green onion
1½ ounce Belvedere vodka
½ ounce lemon juice
¾ ounce simple syrup
2 dashes Angostura bitters
green onion, for garnish

Add tomato and onion into a mixing glass. Muddle, gently, until the mixture is pulpy and fragrant. Add vodka, lemon juice, simple syrup, bitters, and ice cubes. Shake vigorously and strain into a pre-chilled martini glass. Garnish with segment of green onion.

ESCABECHE DE PESCADO IN AVOCADO CUPS

MAKES 6 SERVINGS

Halibut is cubed, marinated, and "cooked" in citrus juice and mixed with sweet onions, spicy peppers, vibrant herbs, and crunchy vegetables. "Bright summer flavors are served in a creamy halved avocado," explains the chef, "Everything is ice cold and not a single burner is ignited!" The dish's acidity complements the sweet and savory aspects of the culinary-inspired cocktail, whose herbal notes mingle with coconut milk dressing.

★ ★ ★ ★ ★

For the dressing:

1 (14-ounce) can unsweetened coconut milk
¼ freshly pressed lime juice
1 lemongrass stalk
2 tablespoons fresh ginger, peeled and minced

Combine the coconut milk and lime juice in a small sauce pot. Smash the lemongrass with the back of a knife and add to the coconut milk with the ginger and bring to a simmer. Simmer for 20 minutes or until reduced slightly and thickened. Remove from the heat and let sit for 30 minutes to infuse. Strain and chill.

For the dish:

3 cups fresh halibut filet, diced
1 cup freshly pressed lime juice
1 tablespoon salt
¼ red onion, shaved thin
¼ cup fresh cilantro leaves
½ red bell pepper, seeded and julienned
½ yellow bell pepper, seeded and julienned
1 jalapeño, seeded and julienned
coconut dressing (from above)
3 avocadoes, cut in half with pits removed
6 sprigs cilantro, for garnish

Combine halibut, lime juice, and salt. Let sit in the refrigerator until cured, approximately 45 minutes. Drain well and reserve. Combine the halibut, coconut dressing, onion, peppers, and cilantro in a bowl and mix well. Just before serving, cut avocados in half and remove their pits. (To prevent the avocados from wobbling when you fill them, make a small cut on the skin side of each avocado parallel to the cut side).

Fill avocados with the mixture. Garnish with cilantro sprigs and serve with plantain chips.

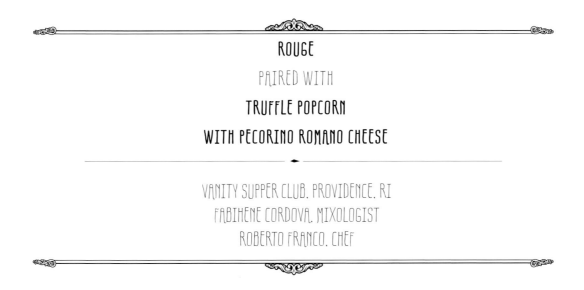

ROUGE

PAIRED WITH

TRUFFLE POPCORN
WITH PECORINO ROMANO CHEESE

VANITY SUPPER CLUB, PROVIDENCE, RI
FABIHENE CORDOVA, MIXOLOGIST
ROBERTO FRANCO, CHEF

In the old days, theater owners would pump in the fragrant aroma of popcorn to attract moviegoers who were, of course, powerless to resist. Truffle-infused oil takes this snack up a notch. Cozy up to watch a movie at home with a batch of this delectable popcorn, an experience made even more pleasurable with a sultry cocktail.

ROUGE

MAKES 1 SERVING

Tart and refreshingly light in the mouth, lemon juice combines with a rye that's brisk, vibrant, and loaded with spice. Red wine crowns the drink with notes of black cherry, black currant, and blackberry. Bright flavors of the cocktail play off saltiness of the Romano and contrast with the weight and crunch of truffle oil and butter–tossed popcorn.

★ ★ ★ ★ ★

2 ounces Bulleit 95 Rye
1 ounce freshly pressed lemon juice
1 ounce simple syrup
½ ounce Cabernet Sauvignon

Combine rye, lemon juice, and simple syrup with ice in a shaker. Shake vigorously and strain into a rocks glass filled with fresh ice. Gently pour the red wine over the back of a spoon held just above the drink's surface so wine floats on top.

TRUFFLE POPCORN
WITH PECORINO ROMANO CHEESE

MAKES 2 SERVINGS

It is said that the pungent scent of truffles is a combination of the memory of lost youth and old love affairs. Infused with white truffles, the olive oil bathes the popcorn with intense earthy aromatics, enhanced with the tang of sheep's cheese and bold blend of Mediterranean spices. Be certain to toss truffle oil with the popcorn while its hot. The heat from the popcorn opens up the intoxicating whiff of truffles.

★ ★ ★ ★ ★

½ cup yellow kernel popcorn, popped
¼ unsalted butter, melted
¼ cup white truffle oil
1 cup freshly grated Pecorino Romano cheese
Italian seasoning, to taste

Place popcorn in a large bowl; add butter and truffle oil and toss to coat. Add cheese and Italian seasoning; toss to combine.

MAIN PLATE PAIRINGS

APPLES TO APRICOT

PAIRED WITH

SEARED MAINE SEA SCALLOPS
WITH SWEET CORN SOUP

MISTRAL KITCHEN, SEATTLE, WA
AMBER JOHANNSON, MIXOLOGIST
WILLIAM BELICKIS, CHEF

Scallops are a sweet, succulent, and meaty shellfish that pair perfectly with fruit flavors. This is an inspired union of seared sea scallops in a corn-based broth served with a cocktail dominated by two fruit-forward spirits: brandy made from French Normandy apples and a liqueur made from Austrian Klosterneuberger apricots.

APPLES TO APRICOTS

MAKES 1 SERVING

"My favorite wine pairing with this dish is a very fruity yet elegant Viognier like a Condrieu from Michel Chapoutier," explains Ms. Johannson. "That's my frame of reference for the blend of spirits—stonefruit flavors from the Calvados and apricot liqueur, brisk nutty notes from the sherry, and bright acid from grapefruit. The barrel-aged Old Tom gin provides an oaky background note that I like with the sweetness and salinity of the scallops."

★★★★★

¾ ounce Château du Breuil "La Pommière" Calvados
½ ounce Ransom Old Tom Gin
¼ ounce Rothman & Winter Orchard Apricot Liqueur
¼ ounce Amontillado sherry
¼ ounce grapefruit juice
¼ ounce simple syrup
dried apricot slice, soaked in Calvados, for garnish

Combine the Calvados, gin, apricot liqueur, sherry, grapefruit juice, and simple syrup with ice in a shaker. Shake vigorously and double-strain into a pre-chilled coupe. Garnish with the dried apricot.

SEARED MAINE SEA SCALLOPS
WITH SWEET CORN SOUP

MAKES 4 SERVINGS

Sea scallops bathe in a rich corn "soup," whose naturally sweet, nutty, buttery flavors form a lovely backdrop, inviting sips of the spirited partner—one of corn's greatest charms is how well it plays with others. The secret to perfectly seared scallops is very high heat for a short amount of time. To avoid overcooking, sear the scallops quickly in a very hot pan; a crust should form on the outside before the inside toughens.

★ ★ ★ ★ ★

1 tablespoon minced shallots
4 tablespoons unsalted butter
6 ears corn (cleaned)
4 cups vegetable stock
16 large sea scallops
salt and pepper, to taste
minced tarragon, for garnish
minced mint, for garnish

In a medium saucepan over medium heat, sauté shallots in 2 tablespoons of butter until translucent. Add the corn kernels and vegetable stock and cook for about 5 minutes. Transfer to a food processor and blend to a smooth consistency. Strain and set aside. Heat a nonstick skillet over high heat and add 2 tablespoons butter. Pat the scallops dry and place in the pan in a single, uncrowded layer. Season with salt and pepper and let sear until one side is browned and crisp, about 2 minutes. Using tongs, turn the scallops and sear the other side, about 2 minutes. Remove pan from the heat and transfer four scallops to each of four warmed shallow bowls. Pour the corn soup into the bowls surrounding the scallops and garnish with the fresh herbs.

THE WILBUR MARY

PAIRED WITH

BISON BURGER

WITH CHARRED TOMATO BARBEQUE SAUCE

TAVERN ON SOUTH, INDIANAPOLIS, IN
KENNY GARDNER, MIXOLOGIST
ALLEN SHIDELER, CHEF

It is said to have originated at Harry's New York Bar in Paris, a magnet for thirsty expatriates during the dry days of Prohibition. Whether or not he was the first person who ever united vodka and tomato juice, a barman there by the name of Fernand Petiot christened the drink a "Bloody Mary." That cocktail masterwork proved to be only the tip of the oeuvre, as evidenced by Mr. Gardner's "designer Bloody Mary" and the ambitious pairing it inspires.

THE WILBUR MARY

MAKES 1 SERVING

Never have tomato and bacon been set in such complementary fashion as by Messers Gardner and Shideler. Bacon flavor underscores the tangy-sweet, full flavor of ripe tomatoes, seasoned with onion, garlic, and peppers for a spicy kick and hints of smoke lingering on the finish. The cocktail covers nearly the full range range of human taste sensations—sweet, salty, sour, and umami or savory—straddling the boundary between food and drink.

★★★★★

For the infused vodka:

1 (750 ml) bottle vodka
½ bunch cilantro
3 tomatoes, quartered
2 garlic cloves, halved
2 chipotle peppers, seeds removed
1 small red onion, sliced into 4 rounds
1 cup of rendered bacon fat
1 cup of water

Add vodka, cilantro, tomatoes, garlic, peppers, and onion to a clean, air-tight jar and store in a cool, dark place for 4 days. Use a fine strainer or paper coffee filter to strain the vodka into another clean jar or bowl and combine with the bacon fat. Infuse for 2 hours or until fat solidifies at the top. Discard the solidified fat and set finished infusion aside until ready to use.

For the drink:

1½ ounces infused vodka (from above)
2 ounces smoked tomato water*
dash bitters
dash Worcestershire sauce
salt and pepper mix, to rim the glass
½ slice bacon, for garnish

Moisten the rim of a highball glass, turn upside down and dip in equal parts of salt and pepper. Combine the infused vodka, smoked tomato water, bitters, and Worcestershire in a shaker with ice. Shake vigorously and strain the contents into the glass over fresh ice. Garnish with bacon slice set across the rim of the glass.

*Hickory-smoke three tomatoes for an hour, then purée with one cup of water.

BISON BURGER

WITH CHARRED TOMATO BARBEQUE SAUCE

MAKES 4 SERVINGS

Here is where the chef matches wits with the barman. His lean, hickory-smoked bison is topped with peppery bacon, a sweet and savory barbecue sauce, ripe tomato, thinly-sliced onion, red leaf lettuce, and a slice of dill pickle, then mounted on toasted brioche. With tomatoes as common protagonist, the burger and cocktail both share overtones of hickory smoke, savory bacon, and aromatic pepper. They work like two clocks in agreement, though entirely independent of one another.

★ ★ ★ ★ ★

For the barbeque sauce:

1 cup red wine vinaigrette
1 large tomato, charred on the grill
1 ounce honey
1 ounce brown sugar
1 ounce chopped onion
2 cups diced tomato
1 teaspoon black pepper
1 teaspoon coriander
1 teaspoon chili powder
1 teaspoon paprika
½ teaspoon cumin
½ teaspoon celery salt
3 ounces cold water
1 ounce corn starch

Purée the red wine vinaigrette, charred tomato, honey, brown sugar, and onion. Transfer to a saucepan over medium-high heat and reduce the purée by half. Remove from heat and add the diced tomato, black pepper, coriander, chili powder, paprika, cumin, and celery salt. Make a slurry with the water and cornstarch and add it to the purée. Cook for another 5 minutes, then remove from heat and blend in a blender until smooth.

For the burgers:

4 (8-ounce) bison burger patties
4 brioche buns
8 slices peppered bacon
4 slices tomato
4 pieces red leaf lettuce
4 slices red onion
4 slices dill pickle
barbeque sauce (from above)

Hickory-smoke the bison burger patties in a smoker for one hour. Remove from the smoker and char-grill to medium-rare. To serve, set the burgers on grilled brioche buns, and top with two slices of peppered bacon, charred tomato sauce, lettuce, tomato, onion, and pickle.

Fireside 75 and Bourbon-Glazed Chicken & Waffles

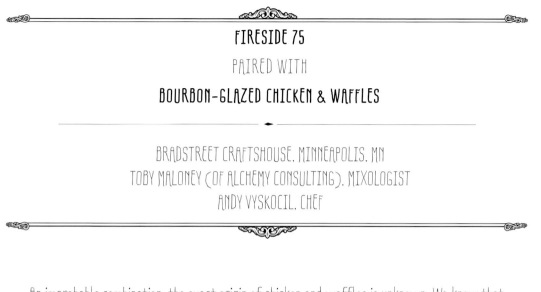

FIRESIDE 75

PAIRED WITH

BOURBON-GLAZED CHICKEN & WAFFLES

BRADSTREET CRAFTSHOUSE, MINNEAPOLIS, MN
TOBY MALONEY (OF ALCHEMY CONSULTING), MIXOLOGIST
ANDY VYSKOCIL, CHEF

An improbable combination, the exact origin of chicken and waffles is unknown. We know that waffles entered American cuisine in the 1790s after Thomas Jefferson's purchase of a waffle iron from France, but it was not until the Jazz Age, when gigs would last until the early hours of the morning, that nightclub musicians invented the combo. Hungry after a long night of performing, they would order plates of fried chicken, and since it was nearly time for breakfast, waffles were served alongside.

FIRESIDE 75

Ignoring cocktail aficionados who debate whether a French 75 is more properly made with gin or cognac, Mr. Maloney combines both spirits in his homage to the classic libation. The blend of botanicals in the gin mingles with musky, spicy flavors in the cognac. In further deviation, maple syrup replaces sugar, thereby matching the dish. "A shared ingredient, maple syrup ties the two together surely, but they also complement each other perfectly," explains the drinksmith. "Not too sweet, nor tart or spicy, they become warm and comfortable like a favorite pair of jeans."

★ ★ ★ ★ ★

½ ounce Beefeater gin
½ ounce Pierre Ferrand Amber Cognac
½ ounce freshly pressed lemon juice
½ ounce maple syrup
3 dashes Fee's Whiskey Barrel Bitters
champagne
orange peel medallion, for garnish

Place a champagne flute in the freezer and chill at least 2 hours. Combine the gin, cognac, lemon juice, maple syrup, and bitters with ice in a shaker. Shake vigorously, then strain into the pre-chilled flute. Top up with the champagne.

BOURBON-GLAZED CHICKEN AND WAFFLES

MAKES 4 SERVINGS

Sandwiched between fluffy waffles and finished with the bourbon maple glaze, the result is a sweet and savory masterpiece. "Chicken and waffles are a dynamic culinary duo," says the chef, "and a cocktail pairing lends to even more fascinating interplay."

★ ★ ★ ★ ★

For the bourbon maple glaze:

⅔ cup orange juice
⅓ cup maple syrup
2 tablespoons bourbon
2 tablespoons brown sugar
1 tablespoon Dijon mustard

Combine the ingredients in a small saucepan over medium heat, whisking to combine. Bring to a simmer, stirring occasionally, until thickened and reduced by about one-third, about 10 minutes. Set aside.

For the dish:

1 (8-ounce) chicken breast
salt
black pepper, freshly cracked
½ cup buttermilk
1 yellow onion, thinly sliced
1 cup seasoned flour
4 mini waffles (cooked)
4 slices apple-wood smoked bacon, cooked and sliced in half

Cut chicken breast into 2-ounce cutlets. Season with salt and pepper. Soak cutlets in the buttermilk and onion overnight. Double dredge the cutlets in the seasoned flour (wet, dry, wet, dry), and then deep fry. Place a cutlet on each waffle, and spoon bourbon glaze over each. Arrange two pieces of bacon on top and serve.

SARSAPARILLA OLD FASHIONED

PAIRED WITH

YAK MEATLOAF

WITH CHIPOTLE MASHED POTATOES

THE COWGIRL, SANTE FE, NM
COLIN NOHL, MIXOLOGIST
PATRICK LAMBERT, CHEF

The drink called sarsaparilla made its debut as a patent medicine, an easy-to-take form of sassafras first marketed in 1885 as a remedy for hangovers and headaches. "In Hollywood westerns, ordering sarsaparilla in a saloon (instead of whiskey) is often met with mockery by the hard-drinking cowboys nearby," explains Mr. Nohl. His cocktail combines Blanton's Single-Barrel Bourbon with sarsaparilla-inspired Root Organic Liqueur and stands up to a manly meatloaf of yak.

SARSAPARILLA OLD FASHIONED

Infused with anise, allspice, cardamom, cinnamon, spearmint, lemon, clove, nutmeg, sugar cane, and birch bark, Root Organic Liqueur has an herbal profile reminiscent of nineteenth-century sarsaparilla. It is spiked with a smoky, woodsy bourbon whiskey that displays hints of brown sugar, honey, and maple syrup. This Old Fashioned-style cocktail's audacious complexity finds favor with big flavors from the kitchen.

★ ★ ★ ★ ★

1 cube sugar
1 slice orange
1 cocktail cherry
½ ounce Root Organic Liqueur
1 ounce Blanton's Single-Barrel Bourbon
club soda

Combine the sugar cube, orange, and cherry with 1 teaspoon of water in an Old Fashioned glass. Muddle gently, until the mixture is pulpy. Add liqueur and whiskey, and stir. Add ice cubes and a splash of club soda. Serve with a swizzle stick.

YAK MEATLOAF

WITH CHIPOTLE MASHED POTATOES

MAKES 4 TO 6 SERVINGS

The chef adds some excitement to a tried-and-true dinner staple by mixing traditional beef with exotic yak meat. But he doesn't stop there. Strong flavors in the cocktail demand an equally complex dish, so he puts chipotle powder in both the meatloaf and potatoes, finding harmony with the spice-rich liqueur and the smoky notes of the bourbon.

★ ★ ★ ★ ★

For the mashed potatoes:

1½ pounds Yukon Gold potatoes, peeled and diced
4 tablespoons heavy cream, at room temperature
2 tablespoons butter, melted
1 teaspoon chipotle powder
1 tablespoon whole milk

Add potatoes to a large saucepan with enough water to cover. Bring to boil, reduce heat, and simmer, covered, for 15 minutes. Drain potatoes and place into a bowl. Add cream, butter, and chipotle powder. Use potato masher to mash potatoes, adding milk to achieve desired consistency.

For the meatloaf:

1½ pounds ground yak
1½ pounds ground beef
1 diced onion
⅔ cup diced celery
1 ounce granulated garlic powder
1 teaspoon dried thyme
1 teaspoon chipotle powder
1 teaspoon kosher salt
1 teaspoon sage
1 teaspoon cumin
4 tablespoons Worcestershire sauce
⅔ cup panko bread crumbs
1 egg
½ cup ketchup

Preheat oven to 350°F. In a large bowl, use your clean hands to combine all ingredients (except the ketchup). Press mixture into a loaf pan with 2-inch-high sides, or form the mixture into a free-standing loaf and place in a rimmed roasting pan. Cover the loaf with the ketchup. Bake for about 1 hour, or until the internal temperature of the meatloaf reaches 155°F. Let rest for 10 minutes. Then gently remove by lifting with a spatula to a serving plate, and slice to serve.

The Brandy Bishop and Veal Tournedos Chantal

THE BRANDY BISHOP

PAIRED WITH

VEAL TOURNEDOS CHANTAL

ARNAUD'S RESTAURANT AND FRENCH 75 BAR, NEW ORLEANS, LA
CHRIS HANNAH, MIXOLOGIST
TOMMY DIGIOVONNI, CHEF

British writer Roy Andries de Groot once described cognac as "a sense of amusement, charm, excitement, all combined into the purest of pleasure." Each component in this sophisticated, cognac-centric cocktail plays with the restaurant's signature dish Veal Tournedos in a different way. From one of the most famous names in the long history of New Orleans dining, this is a pairing meant for tasting, sipping, and thinking.

THE BRANDY BISHOP

MAKES 1 SERVING

Cognac usually conjures images of tweed-clad gentlemen swirling snifters in smoke-filled rooms, When mixed instead of sipped, it provides a genteel accompaniment—and counterbalance—to a delicious dish which has been on Arnaud's menu for over twenty years.

★★★★★

1 ounce cognac
¾ ounce Pisco
¾ ounce red wine–cardamom syrup*
½ ounce lime juice
½ ounce pear juice
1 cocktail cherry or cranberry, for garnish

Combine all liquid ingredients with ice in a shaker. Shake vigorously and strain into a pre-chilled cocktail glass. Garnish with cocktail cherry or cranberry.

*Simmer 3 cups full-bodied red wine (such as an Australian Syrah or a Southern Rhone), 6 ounces light brown sugar, and 3 ounces whole cracked cardamom pods in a sauce pan for 25 minutes. Let cool and strain, discarding the cardamom. Pour into a container and keep refrigerated until ready to use.

VEAL TOURNEDOS CHANTAL

MAKES 4 SERVINGS

The gamey veal and the creamy mushroom sauce are balanced with the tannins and acid of the cocktail's bold wine syrup. "Rather than work against the nature of an ingredient," says Mr. DiGiovonni, "I try to play on the strength of a flavor and use it to my advantage." At Arnaud's, the veal dish is served with herb risotto.

★ ★ ★ ★ ★

For the Chantal sauce:

2 tablespoons unsalted butter
1 ounce shitake mushrooms, sliced
1 ounce oyster mushrooms, sliced
1 ounce medium silver mushrooms, sliced
2 tablespoons shallots, finely diced
½ cup white wine
2 cups heavy cream
2 tablespoons veal stock, reduced to glace stage
1 teaspoon black pepper, freshly cracked
1 teaspoon kosher salt
juice of 1 lemon
2 tablespoons cold unsalted butter

Heat butter in a sauce pan over medium heat. Add shallots and cook until translucent. Add mushrooms and stir well. Cook well until almost all water from mushrooms has been extracted. Add wine and cook until almost dry. Add cream and bring to a boil. Add veal stock, salt, and pepper, and reduce until you can coat the back of a spoon. Add lemon juice and mount with cold butter. Reserve warm for dish.

For the dish:

*9 (3-ounce) portions of veal tournedos
taken from the loin
1 teaspoon kosher salt
1 teaspoon black pepper, freshly
cracked
2 tablespoons clarified butter
Chantal sauce (from above)
3 ounces prepared herb risotto
4 sprigs parsley*

Preheat oven to 450°F. Season tournedos with salt and pepper. Sauté in hot sauté pan with clarified butter until brown on both sides. Place pan in the oven until desired temperature is achieved (medium-rare suggested). Remove from pan and place on warmed plate along with risotto. Spoon Chantal sauce over the tournedos of veal. Garnish each with a sprig of parsley.

TONGUE TIED

PAIRED WITH

SALT & PEPPER WOOD-FIRED PORK RIBS WITH SABA

CRUDO, PHOENIX, AZ
MICAH OLSON, MIXOLOGIST
CULLEN CAMPBELL, CHEF

Rack of ribs, that big slab of porky goodness cut from the shoulder of the hog, is laced with fat and needs slow, low-temperature cooking. Cooked over a wood fire, these ribs take on the flavor of smoke, and find a spirited sidekick in the accompanying cocktail.

TONGUE TIED

MAKES 1 SERVING

The drink combines Italian amaro with Mexican mezcal for a Spaghetti Western-style cocktail that is softened with a muddled fresh strawberry. Mr. Olson engages the bitter edge of herbal liqueur to mellow the peppery, salty notes of the meat and the smoky nature of mezcal to accentuate the dish's aromatics.

★ ★ ★ ★ ★

1 whole strawberry, stem removed
1 ounce Luxardo Abano Amaro
1 ounce Sombra Mezcal
¾ ounce freshly pressed lime juice
¾ ounce simple syrup
strawberry slice, for garnish

Add strawberry and simple syrup into a mixing glass. Muddle, gently, until the mixture is equal parts juice and solids. Add amaro, mezcal, and lime juice. Shake vigorously with ice for 6 seconds. Double strain into a pre-chilled cocktail coupe. Garnish with strawberry slice.

SALT & PEPPER WOOD-FIRED PORK RIBS WITH SABA

MAKES 4 TO 6 SERVINGS

"When pairing dishes and cocktails, we try to balance salt, sugar, and acid," explains Chef Campbell. "We try to make sure that neither partner overwhelms the other, so in this dish I use higher acid to cut through the fat on the ribs and slather fruity, sweet saba on the finish." (In Italian, saba is often labeled as *mosto cotto*, which translates into "cooked grape juice.")

★ ★ ★ ★ ★

2 tablespoons kosher salt
2 tablespoons black pepper, freshly cracked
1 tablespoon chili powder
3 tablespoons brown sugar
2 racks pork ribs (3 pounds each)
6 oz saba (unfermented grape juice)
2 ounces fresh parsley
2 ounces fresh rosemary
2 ounces fresh basil

Preheat oven to 250°F. Combine dry ingredients together in a mixing bowl and coat ribs with the mixture. Place ribs in baking pan, and cover with foil. Place pan in the oven for 2 hours. Remove from oven and grill over a wood fire for 1 hour. (Make sure to lay ribs around the fire so no flames are hitting them directly). After the ribs come off the grill, place them on a serving platter and coat with the saba using a pastry brush. Rough chop all the herbs, combine, and garnish ribs before serving.

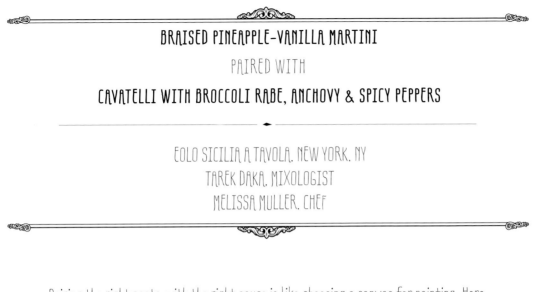

BRAISED PINEAPPLE-VANILLA MARTINI
PAIRED WITH
CAVATELLI WITH BROCCOLI RABE, ANCHOVY & SPICY PEPPERS

EOLO SICILIA A TAVOLA, NEW YORK, NY
TAREK DAKA, MIXOLOGIST
MELISSA MULLER, CHEF

Pairing the right pasta with the right sauce is like choosing a canvas for painting. Here, cavatelli is the ideal shape and texture for a salty, spicy sauce. The accompanying cocktail provides a graceful counterpoint to the rustic flavors. Sweet pineapple balances salty anchovies and olives, while vanilla soothes the heat of spicy peppers.

BRAISED PINEAPPLE-VANILLA MARTINI

MAKES 1 SERVING

The vodka martini is the perfect vehicle for infusions and festive combinations of juices. Vodka itself disappears entirely into its surroundings in this vanilla-perfumed, fruit-forward sipper. (The wide mouth of a classic martini glass helps coax out the drink's bouquet.)

★ ★ ★ ★ ★

1½ ounce pineapple-infused vodka*
1 ounce braised pineapple-vanilla purée**
1 teaspoon freshly squeezed lemon juice
1 thin slice of fresh pineapple, for garnish

Combine the infused vodka, pineapple purée, and lemon juice with crushed ice in a shaker. Shake vigorously and double-strain into a pre-chilled martini glass. Garnish with pineapple slice.

*For the infused vodka: Cut off the top and bottom of 1 pineapple with a sharp knife, making a stable flat base; stand the pineapple upright and remove the skin. Cut fruit into cubes and place in a large glass jar. Add the contents of a 750-milliliter bottle of premium vodka to cover the fruit. Allow to sit for 3 to 4 days. Strain and refrigerate.

**For the pineapple-vanilla purée: Cut pineapple in the same fashion as that used for the infused vodka. In a saucepan, braise the pineapple and 1 vanilla bean with 2 cups of water and 1½ cups of dark rum. (If the pineapple is underripe, add 2 to 4 tablespoons of sugar.) Cook for 1 hour, or until the pineapple is very soft. Remove the vanilla bean and purée the braised pineapple in a blender. Strain through a fine mesh chinois to remove any remaining chunks. Let cool.

CAVATELLI WITH BROCCOLI RABE, ANCHOVY & SPICY PEPPERS

MAKES 4 SERVINGS

The chef owes her passion for cavatelli to the years she spent in rural Sicily as a child. Its small, curled shape and ridged texture are excellent for trapping a sultry sauce that seems to penetrate every taste bud. Serve the pasta "al dente"—meaning "to the tooth"—offering a slight resistance to the bite. (Shop for good-quality broccoli rabe with bright-green leaves that are crisp, upright, and not wilted.)

★ ★ ★ ★ ★

2 bunches broccoli rabe, destemmed, cleaned, and chopped into small pieces
½ pound cavatelli pasta (or any short-cut pasta such as penne or orecchiette)
4 cloves garlic, finely chopped
¾ cup extra virgin olive oil
1 pint ripe cherry tomatoes
6 anchovies, canned, made into a paste
½ cup ripe black Sicilian olives, pitted and halved
6 Italian red peppers (spicy Calabria-style peppers in olive oil), sliced or whole
sea salt

In a pot of boiling, salted water, blanch the broccoli rabe until tender, about 2 minutes. Remove from the pot and place in a bowl of ice water. Cook the pasta until al dente in the same pot of boiling salted water. Meanwhile, in a pan, over low heat, sauté the garlic paste in the extra virgin olive oil. When the garlic is golden, add the cherry tomatoes, squeezing by hand. Add the anchovy paste and let simmer for about 2 minutes. Add the blanched broccoli rabe, olives, and spicy peppers. Spoon some of the oil from the peppers into the sauce, and season with sea salt to taste. When the pasta is al dente, place it in the pan with the sauce. Stir together until the pasta looks like it is well-coated and has absorbed some of the sauce. Serve immediately.

The Witch and Vermouth-and-Fennel Steamed Mussels

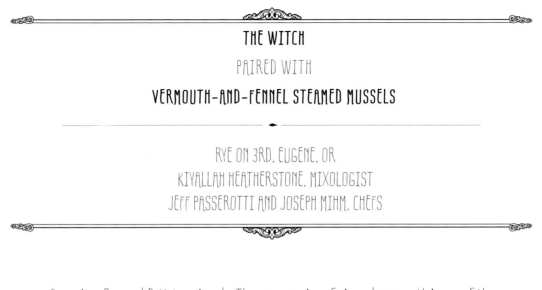

THE WITCH

PAIRED WITH

VERMOUTH-AND-FENNEL STEAMED MUSSELS

RYE ON 3RD, EUGENE, OR
KIYALLAH HEATHERSTONE, MIXOLOGIST
JEFF PASSEROTTI AND JOSEPH MIHM, CHEFS

As writer Bernard DeVoto quipped, "The proper union of gin and vermouth is one of the happiest marriages on earth," referring, of course, to the classic martini. But what if one amorous component appears in a cocktail and the other in an accompanying dish? Will they form a perfect union? The team in Eugene set out to find the answer.

THE WITCH

MAKES 1 SERVING

Combining botanicals of British gin with herbs and spices of Italian Strega, the drink resembles the 1940s-era Joan Crawford cocktail. But with a single dash of a "bewitching" potion, Mr. Heatherstone changes the equation. His secret is celery bitters (Scrappy's is quirky as well as delectable), a seedy, spicy mélange, brightened with hints of citrus. "Two or more dashes is too much," explains the drinksmith. "One dash is perfect."

★ ★ ★ ★ ★

2 ounces London Dry Gin (i.e. Beefeater)
½ ounce Liquore Strega
1 dash Scrappy's Celery Bitters
small celery leaf, for garnish

Combine the gin, Strega, and bitters in a mixing glass filled with ice. Stir to chill and strain into a pre-chilled cocktail glass. Garnish with the celery leaf.

VERMOUTH-AND-FENNEL STEAMED MUSSELS

MAKES 4 SERVINGS

Mussels and vermouth meet in a pot, filled with a few other ingredients, tempting the diner not just to eat the mussels, but also to slurp from the bowl. In the accompanying sipper, Strega, said to be made from seventy different herbs and spices, has strong notes of fennel and pine, connecting to both the gin (with strong juniper) and the fennel in the broth. Savory herbs in the vermouth are enhanced with the kick of celery bitters.

★ ★ ★ ★ ★

25 black mussels (live)
¾ cup Noilly Prat dry vermouth
½ cup shaved fennel
2 teaspoons minced garlic
1 teaspoon finely chopped parsley
1 teaspoon finely chopped thyme
1 teaspoon finely chopped rosemary
2 tablespoons butter

Place sauté pan over heat, hot enough to flame the vermouth. Add mussels, fennel, garlic, and vermouth, give a good stir, cover, and cook for 4 to 5 minutes or until the mussels have opened. After all the mussels have opened, add butter and chopped herbs. Stir, cover, and cook for about 45 more seconds. Serve immediately with crusty bread for dunking.

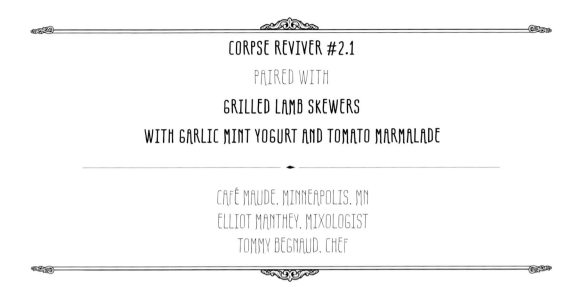

CORPSE REVIVER #2.1

PAIRED WITH

GRILLED LAMB SKEWERS

WITH GARLIC MINT YOGURT AND TOMATO MARMALADE

CAFÉ MAUDE, MINNEAPOLIS, MN
ELLIOT MANTHEY, MIXOLOGIST
TOMMY BEGNAUD, CHEF

Intriguing fragrance of spirits and delicate combination of flavors—it's the alchemy of the Corpse Reviver #.1, so named for its purported ability to bring the dead (or at least painfully hungover) back to some semblance of life. The drink was created in the 1930s by Harry Craddock who, during Prohibition, fled to England where he became chief barman at London's Savoy Hotel. An updated version of the vintage drink makes pals with a punchy and bold dish.

CORPSE REVIVER #2.1

MAKES 1 SERVING

"The Corpse Reviver has a complexity of flavors," explains Mr. Manthey, "yet they work well with one another and with a myriad of flavors in the dish." Delicately balanced, whose taste lingers in the mouth, the drink is updated with Cocchi Americano, an Italian aperitif wine (considered to be the nearest contemporary drink to the original recipe with Kina Lillet), while smooth Mathilde Orange XO substitutes for Cointreau. "We bump up gin in the cocktail as the original recipe is rather sweet," says the drinksmith, "and much like the vintage cocktail, the 2.1 refreshes the palate and enlivens the senses."

★ ★ ★ ★ ★

2 teaspoons absinthe
1½ ounce gin
¾ ounce Cocchi Americano
¾ ounce Mathilde Orange XO
¾ ounce freshly pressed lemon juice

Pour the absinthe into a cocktail glass and swirl to coat the glass; pour out any excess. Combine the gin, Cocci Americano, Mathilde Orange, and lemon juice with ice in a shaker. Shake vigorously and strain into the absinthe-coated glass. Serve without garnish.

GRILLED LAMB SKEWERS

WITH GARLIC MINT YOGURT AND TOMATO MARMALADE

MAKES 8 SERVINGS (3 MEATBALLS PER SERVING)

"The brightness of the cocktail marries with the rich, spicy depth of the lamb," says the chef, "and the cooling palate cleansing of the yogurt and tomato marmalade completes the narrative of this pairing. The mix of spices stands up to the drink's aromatic citrus, juniper, and anise notes."

★ ★ ★ ★ ★

For the yogurt sauce:

2 cups Greek yogurt
10 fresh mint leaves
4 garlic cloves

Combine all ingredients in food processor and pulse to incorporate. Transfer to serving dish.

For the tomato marmalade:

½ cup shallots, minced
1 tablespoon fresh thyme, minced
1 tablespoon canola oil
1 apple, peeled, cored, and diced
2 teaspoons lemon zest
¼ cup honey
2 tablespoons champagne vinegar
1 (28-ounce) can whole plum tomatoes, drained and crushed

Sauté the shallots and thyme in canola oil until soft. Add the apple and lemon zest and continue cooking until apples soften. Add honey and vinegar and cook until mixture reduces by half. Add tomatoes and cook, stirring occasionally, until sauce resembles jam. Remove from heat and transfer to clean bowl to be served as dipping sauce.

For the skewers:

2 ½ pounds ground lamb
¼ cup black currants
½ cup feta cheese, crumbled
2 tablespoons Greek yogurt
¼ cup red onion, finely diced
3 cloves garlic, minced
1 tablespoon fresh cilantro, finely
chopped
1 tablespoon fresh thyme, finely
chopped
1 tablespoon fresh mint, finely chopped
1 teaspoon hot smoked paprika
1 teaspoon cayenne
2 tablespoons harissa (or hot pepper
sauce)
2 teaspoons cumin, toasted and
ground
2 teaspoons coriander, toasted and
ground
2 tablespoons panko breadcrumbs
1 tablespoon kosher salt
2 teaspoons black pepper, freshly
cracked

Combine all ingredients in a large mixing bowl until mixture holds together well. Form into twenty-four 2-ounce balls and thread them onto metal skewers. Place the skewers on an oiled grill rack and grill, turning to brown on all sides, until cooked through, about 8 minutes. Remove the skewers from the grill and serve with the yogurt sauce and tomato marmalade.

Jumbo Scallops with Roasted Red Pepper Chimichurri   New Cuban

NEW CUBAN

PAIRED WITH

JUMBO SCALLOPS
WITH ROASTED RED PEPPER CHIMICHURRI

THE SOCIAL CLUB, MIAMI BEACH, FL
CHAD PHILIPS, MIXOLOGIST
DOUG SISK, CHEF

Rum was once served aboard warships, rationed to visionary explorers, and used to sustain the colonists as they plotted revolution. The Goslings started formulating rum blends in 1860 and developed a dark, full-bodied rum. The name "Black Seal" comes from the wax seal used to reseal champagne bottles discarded by the Royal Air Force officer's club during World War II. Lively notes of caramel, burnt sugar, and butterscotch in the drink make a spirited adventure with jumbo scallops.

NEW CUBAN

MAKES 1 SERVING

Loosely based on Audrey Saunders's Old Cuban (essentially a mojito with Angostura bitters and champagne instead of club soda), Mr. Philips alters the ratios harsh and adds an egg white to smooth out some of the rum's harsh notes. "This is a rich yet easy drinking cocktail," says the drinksmith. "Flavors play together incredibly well and match perfectly with the richness of the scallops and lardon, yet balance out the spiciness of the chimichurri."

★ ★ ★ ★ ★

1 ½ ounces Gosling's Black Seal Rum
¾ ounce freshly pressed lime juice
¾ ounce vanilla bean syrup*
3 leaves fresh mint + 1 small leaf for garnish
1 dash Angostura Bitters + 3 drops for garnish
1 egg white

Combine all ingredients in a shaker. Shake vigorously without ice for 20 to 30 seconds. Add ice and shake vigorously for an additional 20 to 30 seconds. Strain into a pre-chilled martini glass. Garnish with swirled bitters and mint leaf.

*Make simple syrup (1 part water to 1 part white sugar). Split 1 vanilla bean down the middle, cut in half, and place in the simple syrup. Let sit overnight.

JUMBO SCALLOPS

WITH ROASTED RED PEPPER CHIMICHURRI

MAKES 4 SERVINGS

Thanks to sugarcane, rum is inherently sweeter than most other spirits, making it more conducive to pairing with food. The rum-based cocktail is a natural accompaniment to a salty dish that benefits from a bit of sweetness and spice. The note of vanilla helps tease out the flavor of scallop meat. (Bacon may be substituted for the pork belly.)

★ ★ ★ ★ ★

For the chimichurri:

1 red pepper
8 ounces shallots
8 ounces garlic
3 ounces green onions
3 cups red wine vinegar
2 cups olive oil
2 ounces basil
2 ounces sugar
1 tablespoon cayenne pepper
1 tablespoon cumin

Roast red pepper at 350°F until soft, approximately 20 minutes. In a food processor, combine shallots, garlic, and green onions and blend until smooth. Add the roasted red pepper and blend until smooth. Add remainder of the ingredients and blend until well combined. Set aside.

For the dish:

4 tablespoons olive oil
8 U10 scallops
1 teaspoon kosher salt
4 ounces chimichurri (from above)
4 ounces pork belly, diced and sautéed
until crispy
1 ounce arugula
1 tablespoon freshly pressed lemon juice

Preheat the oven to 450°F. Add 3 tablespoons olive oil to the sauté pan at medium-high heat. Season the scallops with salt and sear for 2 minutes. Turn the scallops over and place in the oven on a baking sheet for 7 minutes. Place 1 ounce of the chimichurri in each of four shallow bowls. Lay two scallops over the sauce. Place pork belly around the scallops. Toss arugula with lemon juice and remaining olive oil and top each plate with a small portion.

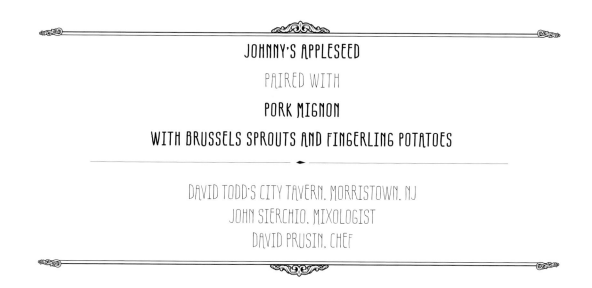

JOHNNY'S APPLESEED

PAIRED WITH

PORK MIGNON

WITH BRUSSELS SPROUTS AND FINGERLING POTATOES

DAVID TODD'S CITY TAVERN, MORRISTOWN, NJ
JOHN SIERCHIO, MIXOLOGIST
DAVID PRUSIN, CHEF

During the Colonial period and up to the middle of the nineteenth century, apple cider was the most popular beverage in America. Cider tradition came to the New World with English settlers, who also brought the custom of pairing apples and pork. Since pigs were slaughtered in the fall and apples were harvested at the same time of year, these two ingredients were naturally used together in the kitchen. The historic match serves as inspiration for a food/cocktail pairing that blurs the lines between sweet and savory.

Johnny's Appleseed and Pork Mignon with Brussels Sprouts and Fingerling Potatoes

JOHNNY'S APPLESEED

MAKES 1 SERVING

The cocktail, assembled with apple-flavored vodka, has cider-like flavors that come from the vanilla/nutmeg syrup and pear purée. The juices of smoky, toothsome pork mingle with sweet and slightly tangy fruit components. There's a warmth to the pairing that almost suggests the smell of a fire in the woodstove.

★ ★ ★ ★ ★

1 ½ ounces Stolichnaya Gala Applik Vodka
¾ ounce vanilla/nutmeg simple syrup*
½ ounce pear purée
3 dashes Angostura bitters
splash freshly pressed lime juice
hard cider, to top up
dried apple slice, for garnish

Combine the vodka, vanilla/nutmeg syrup, pear purée, bitters, and lime juice in a mixing glass filled with ice. Shake vigorously and strain into a 12- to 14-ounce cocktail glass over fresh ice. Garnish with apple slice.

*Add 2 cups granulated sugar, 2 cups water, and 2 teaspoons ground nutmeg into a saucepan over medium heat. Bring to a boil, stirring often. Remove from heat and allow to cool. Add 3 teaspoons vanilla extract and stir to combine. Pour through a fine strainer and store in refrigerator until ready to use.

PORK MIGNON

WITH BRUSSELS SPROUTS AND FINGERLING POTATOES

MAKES 4 SERVINGS

"The cocktail is on the sweet side and tastes similar to an apple pie with a little bite," explains the chef. "This counterbalances the flavorful pork, creating a perfect combination of sweet and savory, and it is precisely because the borders between the different taste sensations are blurring that they become so exciting in the pairing."

★ ★ ★ ★ ★

2 tablespoons canola oil
3 ounces unsalted butter
4 (8-ounce) pork tenderloins
1 pound Brussels sprouts, quartered
1 pound fingerling potatoes, halved lengthwise
1 (4-ounce) tub veal glaze (available at fine supermarkets)
salt
black pepper, freshly cracked

Preheat oven to 400°F. Heat skillet over medium-high heat with the canola oil and 1 ounce of butter. Liberally salt and pepper both sides of the tenderloins. Sear pork on both sides, and place in the oven for approximately 12 minutes or until internal temperature reaches 145°F. Heat sauté pan with 1½ ounces butter. Sauté Brussels sprouts to caramelize. Season with salt and pepper. Remove from pan. Blanch potatoes in salted boiling water, approximately 1 minute. Remove and pat dry. In skillet, heat remaining butter and add potatoes. Season with salt and pepper. Sauté until golden brown. Add tenderloins to four warm plates, drizzle veal glaze over top of each, and serve with Brussels sprouts and potatoes.

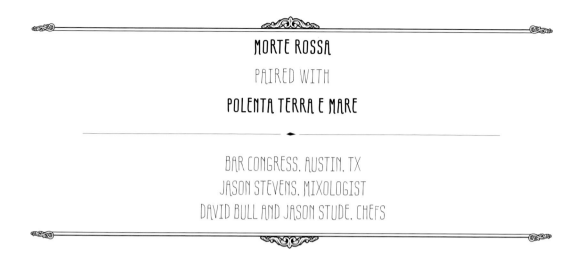

MORTE ROSSA

PAIRED WITH

POLENTA TERRA E MARE

BAR CONGRESS, AUSTIN, TX
JASON STEVENS, MIXOLOGIST
DAVID BULL AND JASON STUDE, CHEFS

"Prosecco gently teases out fruit and spice as it cuts through the richness of the polenta," says the drinksmith. "The dark, blackcurrant fruit plays off the lobster and pork, and the Herbsaint echoes the fennel, firmly tying dish and cocktail together and achieving an incredible harmony of flavors." A mysterious and contemplative drink.

MORTE ROSSA

MAKES 1 SERVING

Two classic cocktails are motivating factors behind the liquid partner in this pairing. Absinthe and champagne are borrowed from "Death in the Afternoon," a cocktail invented by Ernest Hemingway, sharing the name of his book about bullfighting; in the "Kir Royale," a measure of crème de cassis (blackcurrant liqueur) is similarly topped up with champagne.

★ ★ ★ ★ ★

1 ounce Byrrh Grand Quinquina
¼ ounce Cassis de Bourgogne
2 dashes Herbsaint or absinthe
Prosecco
lemon peel medallion

Combine byrrh, cassis, and Herbsaint in mixing glass and stir briefly (without ice) to integrate. Pour into a pre-chilled flute or coupe and top up with the sparkling wine. Squeeze lemon peel over the surface to express oils and drop into the cocktail.

POLENTA TERRA E MARE

MAKES 4 SERVINGS

"The southwestern coast of Italy inspires this dish," explains Mr. Bull. "It is at once refined and comforting. It's spicy and rich, with fennel flavor running throughout. The dish itself is more about expression and comfort than anything else." The small red Calabrese pepper is called "the devil's kiss," and with just a drizzle, the stimulating romesco provides atmospheric background to the creamy polenta.

★ ★ ★ ★ ★

For the Calabrese romesco:

¼ cup Calabrese chile peppers in oil
2 tablespoons Marcona Almonds
1 teaspoon garlic, minced
¼ cup extra virgin olive oil
1 teaspoon sherry vinegar

For the poached eggs:

4 eggs
2 quarts water
1 tablespoon white vinegar

In a small sauté pan, sauté the garlic in the olive oil until slightly toasted. Add all other ingredients into a small food processor. In a slow steady stream, pour in the garlic and olive oil until totally puréed and emulsified. Adjust seasoning with salt.

Crack the eggs into individual ramekins. In a medium saucepot, warm the water and vinegar to a gentle simmer. Using a slotted spoon, stir water in the same direction to create a gentle vortex in the center. Gently drop egg in one by one while continuing to move the water in the same direction (this keeps the eggs from dropping to the bottom of the pan and sticking). Cook the eggs at a very gentle simmer for about 6 minutes for a runny yolk. Remove gently with a slotted spoon.

For the lobster and pork sausage:

2 tablespoons extra virgin olive oil
½ pound pork shoulder, ground
1 tablespoon garlic, minced
1 teaspoon fennel seeds, toasted and ground
pinch garlic powder
pinch dried oregano
pinch black pepper
½ pound lobster meat, cooked and cut to a small dice (tail or claw)
½ teaspoon sea salt
pinch chile flakes

For the pickled fennel salad:

1 fennel bulb
1 cup water
1 cup white vinegar
3 tablespoons sugar
2 tablespoons sea salt

Heat a large skillet or sauté pan over medium-high heat. Pour in the olive oil. Place the ground pork in the pan and cook through. Browning the meat a little will help the flavor. Once the pork is almost cooked, add the garlic and cook for one minute. Add spices and cook for one more minute. Add lobster meat and adjust seasoning and spice with salt and chile flakes.

Bring the water, vinegar, sugar, and salt to a boil, making sure the sugar and salt are completely dissolved. Cut off the top of the fennel and reserve some of the fronds. Peel the fennel bulb and cut into a thin julienne. Place julienned fennel into a small bowl and pour over hot liquid. Cover with plastic wrap and allow mixture to cool. Once cooled, remove fennel from liquid and toss with some of the reserved fennel fronds.

For the polenta:

2 cups heavy cream
2 cups fish stock
1 cup quick cooking polenta
1 tablespoon unsalted butter
2 tablespoons finely diced yellow onion
1 teaspoon minced garlic
1 teaspoon sea salt
1 fresh bay leaf

To assemble:

Warm a medium-sized saucepot over moderate heat. Add butter, onion, garlic, and bay and sweat until translucent, about 5 minutes. Add the heavy cream and stock and bring to a gentle simmer. In a slow, steady stream, whisk polenta into the liquid. Add salt and continue to whisk. Cook at low heat, stirring frequently for about 10 minutes to avoid lumps. Remove bay leaf and adjust seasoning with salt.

Place 1 cup of the polenta in each of four warmed bowls. Top each with ¼ cup of lobster sausage. Make a divit with the back of a spoon and nestle in a poached egg, lightly seasoned with salt and cracked pepper. Dot the romesco around the top and place a pinch of the fennel salad next to the egg.

Potato Pierogi with Citrus Lavender Marmalade

Little Mr. Sunshine

LITTLE MR. SUNSHINE

PAIRED WITH

POTATO PIEROGI
WITH CITRUS LAVENDER MARMALADE

MUD HEN TAVERN, LOS ANGELES, CA
MORGAN FOXX, MIXOLOGIST
SUSAN FENIGER AND KAJSA ALGER, CHEFS

Supposedly, the drink originated at the Paris Ritz during World War I, inspired by an American army captain who rode up to the hotel in a motorcycle sidecar. Pushing the boundary of a classic Sidecar cocktail, the barsmith merges cognac with orange liqueur, then balances tart lemon with sweet, lavender-scented syrup. The tiny purple flowers of the lavender plant provide an interesting give-and-take between the cocktail and its savory accompaniment.

LITTLE MR. SUNSHINE

MAKES 1 SERVING

This potent cocktail could be called a holy trinity of rich, sweet, and tart—featuring aged spirits, lavender-infused syrup, and fresh lemon. The vigorous shake is an "open door" that unlocks floral aromatics of the cognac, lavender, and bitters, and those jazzy notes of citrus provide just enough counterpoise to the savory filling in the dish.

★ ★ ★ ★ ★

2 ounces Hine VSOP Cognac H
½ ounce Mandarine Napoléon
½ ounce lavender simple syrup*
¾ ounce freshly pressed lemon juice
2 dashes of Peychaud's bitters
sprig of fresh lavender, for garnish

Combine cognac, liqueur, simple syrup, lemon juice, and bitters with ice in a shaker. Shake vigorously and strain into a pre-chilled coupe with a half-sugared rim and a sprig of lavender for garnish.

*Combine 1 cup water, 1 cup sugar, and 3 tablespoons dried lavender into saucepan and simmer for 30 minutes. Allow the mixture to cool and then strain and bottle. Refrigerate until ready to use.

POTATO PIEROGI

WITH CITRUS LAVENDER MARMALADE

MAKES 4 TO 6 SERVINGS

Traditionally considered peasant food, pierogi are the most popular dish in Polish cooking, and fans of the delectable dumplings include people of all ethnicities. The Mud Hen version is a playful pairing of potato, lavender, and feta cheese. Potatoes take on a sweet, floral note when combined with lavender, amplified with lush lavender notes in the attendant cocktail.

★ ★ ★ ★ ★

For the potato filling:

2 Yukon Gold potatoes, peeled and cut into 8
4 cups cold water
1½ teaspoons kosher salt
2½ tablespoons olive oil
1 white onion, cut in small dice
5 ounces (1 cup) feta cheese, crumbled

Place the potatoes, water, and 1 teaspoon of the salt in a small saucepot over high heat. Bring to a boil, about 5 minutes. Reduce the heat to medium-low and continue to cook on a slow boil for another 15 minutes, or until potatoes are very tender when poked with a fork. Drain and wait for 5 to 10 minutes, until cool enough to handle. Grate on the large holes of a box grater and then set aside. Meanwhile, heat the olive oil in a large sauté pan over medium-high heat. Add the onions and cook, stirring frequently, until golden brown, about 4 to 5 minutes. Place the potato, sautéed onion, and feta in a bowl and mix gently to combine. Taste for salt and adjust if necessary.

For the marmalade:

2 lemons, washed well

2 seedless oranges, washed well

1 grapefruit, washed well

½ cup water

2 cups granulated sugar

1 tablespoon lavender

½ teaspoon kosher salt

For the pierogi dough:

1 egg, beaten

⅓ cup sour cream

1 pound all-purpose flour (1¾ cups),

plus extra for rolling

1 tablespoon dried lavender

1 teaspoons kosher salt

1 stick (4 ounces) cold, unsalted

butter, cut in small pieces

With a peeler, remove the peels of all the fruit. Thinly slice into delicate strips and place in a small saucepot. Cut off the ends of each fruit and then down the sides, removing the now zested peel (the white pith), so that you are left with just the fruit. Discard the pith.

Cut the fruit into small ½-inch pieces, removing any large pith and seeds. Place all the fruit in the same saucepot with the zest. Add the remaining ingredients and stir well to combine and dissolve the sugar. Place the saucepot over medium heat for 5 minutes, stirring occasionally, until mixture boils. Reduce heat slightly and let simmer for 20 to 25 minutes, until thick and glossy. Remove from heat, stir in lavender, and transfer into a container to cool in the refrigerator.

In a small bowl, mix the egg and sour cream together. Set aside. Place the flour, lavender, and salt in a stand mixer with paddle attachment. Start on slow speed, adding the butter one piece at a time until the flour starts to come together in small clumps, about 2 minutes. Stop the mixer and add the egg and sour cream mixture all at once to the mixing bowl. Turn on the mixer again, at slow speed and mix just enough to incorporate the sour cream mixture. (Do not overmix or your dough will be tough.) The consistency will be slightly crumbly, and resemble a pie dough. Turn off mixer and place dough on a flat surface. Knead with your hands slightly, just enough to bring the dough together into a small ball. Wrap in plastic wrap and refrigerate for at least 1 hour, until cool. Divide the dough in half. Place one half at a time on a flat surface, sprinkled with flour for rolling. Roll to a thickness of approximately 1/8 inch. Cut into circles with a round cookie cutter with a 3-inch diameter. Roll and cut until all of your circles are cut. Place the circles on a plate in the refrigerator and set aside until ready to use.

For the dish:

water, for boiling
24 pierogi dough circles (from above)
3 cups potato filling (from above)
6 tablespoons butter, for searing
1 cup sour cream
1 cup citrus lavender marmalade
(from above)
4 tablespoons chopped parsley, for
garnish

Place a large pot of water on the stove to boil. Put a level tablespoon of filling in the center of each dough circle. Fold the dough into a half-moon shape and, making sure that the filling doesn't squeeze out, press the edges together firmly with your fingers to hold together. (The dough is pliable, so if there seems too much filling, you can stretch the dough a little bit to fit around it). Repeat until all the dumplings are filled.

Boil the dumplings for 3 minutes and then drain, being careful that they don't tear. Melt the butter in a large sauté pan. When frothy, add the dumplings in so that they lie in a single layer. (You may have to do this step in two or three batches depending on the size of your pan). Cook for just 1 to 2 minutes on each side, so that they have a light golden brown sear and are slightly crispy but not fully browned or fried. Spread a heavy spoonful of sour cream across the center of each plate. Follow with a spoonful of citrus marmalade. Place the dumplings for each guest across the sour cream and marmalade and top with some chopped parsley before serving.

HIGHBURY COCKTAIL

PAIRED WITH

FLOUNDER "MUFFULETTA"

PARLOR MARKET, JACKSON, MS
JOHN INGRAM, MIXOLOGIST
MATTHEW KAJDAN, CHEF

The dish is inspired by an old farmer's market tradition in the French Quarter of New Orleans, where a Sicilian "farmer's lunch" consisted of cured meats, cheese, and olive salad piled onto a sturdy Italian bread called muffuletta. The key ingredient is the olive mix, whose tanginess boosts the flounder's flavor and complements the more savory characteristics of a gin-based cocktail.

HIGHBURY COCKTAIL

MAKES 1 SERVING

There is much to admire in Mr. Ingram's composition. The cocktail builds on its base of juniper, coriander, and cucumber. Hendrick's—a gin that stands up for itself—resonates with piquant blackcurrant concentrate, ginger spice, mint essence, fresh citrus, and a hint of bitters.

★ ★ ★ ★ ★

5 leaves fresh mint
2 shakes Dr. Adam Elmegirab's
dandelion & burdock bitters
2 ounces Hendrick's gin
½ ounce freshly pressed lemon juice
½ ounce Ribena (blackcurrant syrup)
¼ ounce Domain de Canton ginger
liqueur
mint sprig, for garnish

Add the mint leaves and bitters into a mixing glass. Muddle, gently, to express the mint oils. Add the gin, lemon juice, Ribena, ginger liqueur, and ice cubes. Shake vigorously and double-strain into a pre-chilled cocktail coupe. Garnish with the mint sprig.

FLOUNDER "MUFFULETTA"

MAKES 4 SERVINGS

The muffuletta remains a hearty grab-and-go New Orleans lunch favorite. Chef Kajdan deconstructs the muffuletta's mingled filling and reassembles its ingredients in a fish dish to accompany the cocktail. "They are both somewhat complex," he explains, "yet they are both light and refreshing on the palate."

★ ★ ★ ★ ★

For the olive mix:

½ cup pimento-stuffed olives
¼ cup Kalamata olives, pitted
¼ cup giardiniera pickled vegetables
2 pepperoncini
4 pickled onions
2 tablespoons capers
1 clove garlic, chopped
1 teaspoon dried oregano
2 teaspoons freshly pressed lemon juice
2 tablespoons olive oil

Drain and place all ingredients in a food processor and pulse until coarsely chopped.

For the emulsion:

4 egg yolks
2 tablespoons Dijon mustard
5 anchovy filets
½ cup parmesan
1 cup olive oil
3 tablespoons lemon juice
1 tablespoon Worcestershire sauce
¼ cup minced garlic
3 tablespoons fresh herbs
salt
black pepper, freshly cracked

Blend egg yolks, mustard, garlic, and anchovies in food processor until smooth, then drizzle in olive oil to emulsify. Add remaining ingredients and season with salt and pepper.

For the dish:

2 pints fingerling potatoes
3 cloves garlic, crushed and finely minced
1 teaspoon chopped fresh rosemary
½ teaspoon dried leaf thyme
7 tablespoons olive oil
4 (6-ounce) fresh flounder filets, trimmed, patted dry
salt
black pepper, freshly cracked
½ cup of olive salad (from above)
¼ pound arugula, chopped
¼ pound soppressata, sliced thin
parmesan/anchovy emulsion (from above)

Preheat oven to 225°F. Scrub potatoes and toss with garlic, rosemary, thyme, and 3 tablespoons of olive oil. Arrange potatoes in single layer, not touching, in nonstick roasting pan. Bake until tender, about 1 hour, then cool and slice into disks. Toss potatoes with arugula, soppressata, and emulsion. Set aside. Season filets with salt and pepper. Swirl 3 tablespoons of olive oil to coat the pan, and sear filets over medium-high heat, 2 minutes on each side. Add 1 tablespoon of olive oil on the flip. Prepare each of four plates with a bed of the potato salad and place a flounder filet on top. Dress each with a tablespoon of the olive mix.

"BREAKFAST IN DENVER" BLOODY MARY
PAIRED WITH
FREAKIN' DENVER OMELET

INTERSTATE KITCHEN & BAR, DENVER, CO
JOEY NEWMAN, MIXOLOGIST
ANDRE LOBATO, CHEF

The origin of the Denver omelet can be traced to Chinese immigrants who worked on construction of the transcontinental railroad in the mid-1800s. They created the dish as a sort of American "egg foo yung," first between slices of bread, then as a stand-alone omelet. According to James Beard, "It seems to have been called the Western until the railroads made it to Utah, and then folks in Utah apparently renamed it the Denver." There's something about the way they make Denver omelets in Denver, and Mr. Lobato's version calls for a dolled-up Bloody Mary to wash it down.

"BREAKFAST IN DENVER" BLOODY MARY

MAKES 1 SERVING

Drinking at breakfast is a rare pleasure, one that often includes the time-honored Bloody Mary. In his version, Mr. Newman employs a foundation he calls the "mud mix," an intense medley—terrifying and alluring in equal measure. His cocktail glass is seasoned with herbs and spices and topped with pepperoncini pepper, stuffed queen olive, pickle, lime wedge, and candied bacon. Since it's meant to be sipped rather than glugged, serve without ice to prevent dilution.

★ ★ ★ ★ ★

For the seasoned rim:

1 teaspoon kosher salt
1 teaspoon dried chili flakes
1 teaspoon tomato powder
1 teaspoon ground cayenne pepper
1 teaspoon ground paprika

Mix all ingredients thoroughly and set out on a saucer or plate.

For the "mud" mix:

1 tablespoon Worcestershire sauce
1 tablespoon hot sauce
½ tablespoon pepperoncini pepper juice
1 tablespoon horseradish sauce
½ tablespoon celery seed
½ tablespoon black pepper, freshly cracked
1 tablespoon kosher salt

In a small bowl, blend all ingredients thoroughly. Set aside.

For the candied bacon:

Bake 1 strip of bacon until nearly done, then sprinkle white and brown sugar onto strip. Let bake until sugar has dissolved but not burned.

For the drink:

1 ½ ounces vodka
1 ½ ounces mud mix (from above)
3 ounces tomato juice
lime wedge
rim seasoning (from above)

Wet rim of a cocktail glass with lime wedge. Spin edge of glass in rim seasoning, making sure to evenly and fully coat entire rim. Combine the vodka, mud mix, and tomato juice with ice in a shaker. Shake gently and strain into the seasoned glass. Garnish with pepperoncini pepper, stuffed queen olive, pickle, lime wedge, and candied bacon.

FREAKIN' DENVER OMELET

MAKES 4 SERVINGS

"Nothing goes better for breakfast than a 'bloody' and some eggs," insists Mr. Lobato, who turns near caricature into a vital pairing. "The rejuvenating cocktail has a symbiotic relationship with the savory omelet." The mixture of ham, eggs, potatoes, peppers, and cheese conjures up images of those chuck wagon cooks—comfort food in the morning.

★ ★ ★ ★ ★

4 medium Yukon Gold potatoes, cut into ¼-inch cubes

vegetable oil

½ cup black forest ham, cut into small cubes

1 cup sweet Vidalia onions, finely julienned

1 medium green bell pepper, finely julienned

12 eggs

½ red onion, finely diced

salt

black pepper, freshly cracked

½ cup shredded sharp cheddar

½ cup shredded mozzarella

In medium sauce pot, bring 6 cups water to rolling boil. Add cubed potatoes and cook through, about 4 minutes. Remove sauce pot from heat, drain water, and pat dry. In cast-iron skillet over medium heat, add 2 tablespoons vegetable oil, and brown ham, onion, and bell pepper until ham is crispy and onion is caramelized. Remove skillet from heat, drain fat, and place ingredients on paper towel. In large mixing bowl, beat eggs with balloon whisk to about 1½ of the original volume. In same cast-iron skillet, over high heat, add 2 tablespoons vegetable oil and brown the potatoes, adding red onion when half done. Salt and pepper to taste. Remove from heat when golden brown.

Preheat oven to 350°F. In four medium nonstick pans over medium heat, add 2 tablespoons vegetable oil and ¼ each of the beaten egg. Stir egg until scrambling begins. Turn off heat, add shredded cheeses, ham, bell pepper, and onion. Place pans in oven for about 3 minutes. Place ¼ of potato hash on each of four plates, gently roll each omelet in pan, then move onto the plated hash. Served with buttered toast.

Plantain Polenta with Spicy Tomato Ragu

The Playboy

Kelsey Schulz and Jeremiah Schenzel of the Cocktail Club.

THE PLAYBOY

PAIRED WITH

PLANTAIN POLENTA WITH SPICY TOMATO RAGU

THE COCKTAIL CLUB, CHARLESTON, SC
KELSEY SCHULZ, MIXOLOGIST
JEREMIAH SCHENZEL, CHEF

"The cocktail was the launch pad for the pairing," explains Ms. Schulz, who calls her collaboration with the chef "a meeting of the minds." In building a unique dish around the drink, bartender and chef use the undertones of "heat" as an intermediary in this successful alliance.

THE PLAYBOY

MAKES 1 SERVING

Artful and intriguing, almost a "salad in a glass," the cocktail practically invites the chef to frame it with food. Besides the spicy pepper notes, a bridge is constructed by using ingredients that aren't actually in the drink itself but pair perfectly with the ingredients that are.

★ ★ ★ ★ ★

2 ounces jalapeño-infused vodka*
2 ounces pineapple juice
1 ounce arugula syrup**
½ ounce freshly pressed lime juice
½-inch wheel of cucumber
barbeque-lime salt***

Moisten the rim of a chilled martini glass with a lemon peel and dip into the barbeque-lime salt to coat. Set aside. Place the cucumber wheel into a mixing glass and muddle to a pulp. Add remaining ingredients and fill two-thirds full of ice cubes. Shake vigorously and double-strain into the prepared Martini glass.

*Add 1 jalapeño pepper to a 750-milliliter bottle of vodka. Secure lid and shake three or four times. Place in a cool, dark place for 24 hours or until flavor reaches desired intensity. Strain through a paper coffee filter into a clean container and refrigerate until ready to use.

**Heat 1 cup sugar, 1 cup water, and 1 cup loosely packed arugula leaves over medium heat, stirring occasionally, until sugar has dissolved. Remove from heat, and allow to steep for about 15 minutes. Strain into a clean container and refrigerate until ready to use.

***Combine 1 teaspoon cayenne pepper, 3 tablespoons smoked hot paprika, 6 tablespoons kosher salt, 3 tablespoons brown sugar, and the zest of 2 limes, and let sit overnight to completely dehydrate lime zest.

PLANTAIN POLENTA WITH SPICY TOMATO RAGU

The most apparent relationship between cocktail and dish is the slight burn of jalapeños. Its no more than a little tingle on the tongue in the drink, but it finds easy-going kinship with the spicy sauce. The intermingling of fruit and vegetables appears both in the dish and the cocktail.

★ ★ ★ ★ ★

For the polenta:

2 cups whole milk
2 cups vegetable stock
1 cup polenta
1 ripe plantain

In a medium sauce pot, combine whole milk and vegetable stock. Season with salt and bring to a boil. Reduce heat to low and whisk in polenta. Season, and cook for about 20 minutes or until the graininess of the polenta has dissipated. (Stir frequently to prevent burning on bottom of the pan). Once cooked, smash the plantain and fold into the polenta. Pour the polenta into a 9-inch-square baking dish, greased and lined with parchment paper. Allow to cool overnight in the fridge.

For the sauce:

½ cup diced sweet onions
3 garlic cloves, minced
3 cups chopped tomatoes
½ cup orange juice
4 tablespoons pickled jalapeños,
chopped
salt and pepper, to taste
cooking oil, as needed

Heat a pan over medium heat with approximately 2 tablespoons cooking oil. Add the onions and garlic and cook until onions are translucent. Reduce heat to low and add the tomatoes, cooking until they begin releasing their natural juice. Add the orange juice and reduce the mixture by half. Once reduced, add the pickled jalapeños and season to taste.

To assemble:

Remove the polenta from the baking dish and cut into appropriate-sized portions. Heat a nonstick pan over high heat and add polenta. Cook until edges are lightly golden brown and polenta is heated through. Place polenta portions on warmed serving dishes and spoon the spicy tomato sauce over the top of each.

All Hands on Deck and Grilled Jerk Quail with Banana Rum Jam

ALL HANDS ON DECK
PAIRED WITH
GRILLED JERK QUAIL
WITH BANANA RUM JAM

TABARD INN, WASHINGTON, DC
CHANTAL TSENG, MIXOLOGIST
PAUL PELT, CHEF

The Caribbean has given us jerk cooking and some of the world's finest rum. The spicy-sweet-and-savory jerk experience is like a carnival in the mouth. Aromatic rum has been called "the spice of life" with smooth flavors and a bit of a kick. Jerk dishes go well with something cold and slightly sweet: rum cocktails work because they usually have a measure of fruit to provide some calm.

ALL HANDS ON DECK

MAKES 1 SERVING

The small-batch rum is aged in oak barrels, previously used to age bourbons, rendering notes of spice and toasted wood, followed by fruit. While the base spirit establishes the theme and mirrors the jam, in the dish other components in the drink shrewdly take aim at the jerk spices—fruity Oloroso sherry and allspice-flavored liqueur in particular. "This is a cocktail that draws its influences from the tropical tiki style and as such could easily be made into a punch," says the drinksmith. "Just multiply recipe by the number of guests you wish to serve."

★ ★ ★ ★ ★

1 ounce Mt. Gay Black Barrel Rum
1 ounce Lustau East India Oloroso sherry
¾ ounce Kina L'Avion d'Or
¾ ounce orange juice
dash lemon juice
dash allspice dram
orange peel, for garnish
sprig of fresh mint, for garnish

Combine rum, sherry, aperitif, orange juice, lemon juice, and allspice dram with ice in a shaker. Shake vigorously and strain over fresh ice in a glass mug or punch cup. Garnish with orange peel and mint sprig.

GRILLED JERK QUAIL

WITH BANANA RUM JAM

MAKES 4 SERVINGS

The pairing pivots on the natural affinity of jerk spices and rum; the flow of flavors, from sweet to smoky and with a background of heat, hits just the right notes with the cocktail composition. Subtle sweetness of the bananas works magic in contrast to the spicy jerk, providing sotto voce to "lower the volume" for emphasis.

★ ★ ★ ★ ★

For the dry jerk seasoning:

2 tablespoons cayenne or ground dry chipotle pepper
2 tablespoons onion powder
2 tablespoons granulated garlic
3 tablespoons ground ginger
1 tablespoon black pepper
1 tablespoon dry thyme
2 tablespoons ground allspice
1 tablespoon cinnamon
1 teaspoon ground clove
1 teaspoon nutmeg or mace

Place all ingredients into a very large bowl. Mix together until well blended. Store in airtight container.

For the banana rum jam:

4 cups peeled and diced bananas
6 tablespoons lime juice
2 vitamin C pills, crushed to a powder
5 cups light brown sugar
½ teaspoon butter
1 (3-ounce) pack of pectin
2 tablespoons dark rum

For the dish:

4 quail, rib bones removed
dry jerk seasoning (from above)
salt
mesclun greens
banana rum jam (from above)

Combine banana, lime juice, and vitamin C powder in a large saucepan over high heat. Add sugar and butter and stir until sugar is dissolved. Bring to a boil, add pectin, and boil for an addional 60 seconds. Remove from heat and add rum. Set aside to cool.

Preheat a grill. Season each quail with ½ to 1 tablespoon of jerk seasoning and a pinch of salt. Grill quail to medium-rare with a crispy char. Serve over mesclun greens with the banana rum jam.

PIMM'S BLUE RIBBON

PAIRED WITH

SKATE WING FISH & CHIPS

MEAT & POTATOES, PITTSBURGH, PA
MIKE MILLS, MIXOLOGIST
RICHARD DESHANTZ, CHEF

For the uninitiated, Pimm's (officially, Pimm's No. 1 Cup) was introduced to the British public in 1823 by a London oyster bar owner named James Pimm. The herbal, subtly spicy, gin-based liqueur is traditionally blended over ice with ginger ale or sparkling lemonade, but Mr. Mills puts a twist on the most beloved of British summertime cocktails and forges an alliance with another British classic, fish and chips. Sometimes it takes just one thing to ensure good chemistry. For this pairing, it's PBR.

PIMM'S BLUE RIBBON

MAKES 1 SERVING

The drinksmith builds his shandy-inspired libation with Pimm's, St. Germain elderflower liqueur, lemon juice, and the ubiquitous two-dollar-a-can Pabst Blue Ribbon. The result is lively, playful, yet drier and rounder in flavor than the version served at the All-England Club. "The cocktail can change and grow in gusto by adding more of the beer as you drink it," he explains. "It's fizzy, aromatic, cold, and gently sweet—perhaps the perfect summer-afternoon drink."

★ ★ ★ ★ ★

1½ ounce Pimm's No. 1 Cup
¾ ounce St. Germain
½ ounce freshly pressed lemon juice
½ ounce simple syrup
Pabst Blue Ribbon, to top up
orange peel, for garnish
cucumber slice, for garnish

Combine Pimm's, St. Germain, lemon juice, and simple syrup with ice in a shaker. Shake vigorously and strain into a tall glass over fresh ice. Top up with the PBR and stir gently. Garnish with orange peel and cucumber.

SKATE WING FISH & CHIPS

MAKES 4 SERVINGS

"Beer and seafood are wonderful bedfellows," explains the chef. "The fish and chips dish is citrus and salty and the beer is sweet and grainy—beer seems to tease out the flavor of the fish. Sourness of the malt vinegar is a nice foil to the skate wing flesh: tender, firm, and delicate without being fragile like flounder. And lemon elements refine, refresh, and tie them together."

★ ★ ★ ★ ★

For the malt vinegar aioli:

1 tablespoon minced fresh chives
¼ cup malt vinegar
2 cups mayonnaise

Whisk the chives together with the malt vinegar and mayonnaise. Set aside.

For the mushy peas:

2 cups frozen peas
1 tablespoon chopped mint
½ cup heavy cream

In a medium saucepan, bring the peas, mint, and heavy cream to a simmer. Once heated, purée in a blender. (Do not allow the peas to become completely broken down, to allow some texture.) Keep on low heat until plating.

For the frisée salad:

¼ cup freshly pressed lemon juice
1 cup extra virgin olive oil
2 heads frisée lettuce
1 tablespoon capers

Mix together lemon juice and olive oil. Place frisée and capers in a large serving bowl; toss with the dressing, and set aside until plating.

For the potato chips:

2 Yukon Gold potatoes, sliced paper thin (peel optional)
vegetable oil, for deep frying
salt
black pepper, freshly cracked

For the dish:

2 cups seasoned flour
1 teaspoon salt
½ teaspoon black pepper, freshly cracked
¼ cup water
4 eggs
vegetable oil, for deep frying
1 ½ pounds skate wing, divided into 4 portions
malt vinegar aioli (from above)
potato chips (from above)
frisée salad (from above)

Put the slices into a bowl of cold water and let stand for 1 hour. Deep fry at 350°F until golden brown. Remove from the oil and toss with salt and pepper to taste. Keep warm until ready to serve.

In a bowl, combine the flour, salt, and pepper. Whisk in water and then the eggs. Heat oil in a deep heavy pot over moderately high heat until it registers 350°F on thermometer. Dip each fillet into the batter and place very carefully into the hot oil. Don't crowd the pieces. Flip over with tongs when the edges start to turn light brown. Drain on paper towels. Add a base of the malt vinegar aioli and mushy peas to each of four warmed plates. Place a fried skate wing and a portion of the frisée salad on each. Top with potato chips and serve immediately.

DESSERT PAIRINGS

LAVENDER BEE'S KNEES

PAIRED WITH

LAVENDER GOAT CHEESE TARTLETS

LOCAL, NORMAN, OK
DANA NIXON MOFFER, MIXOLOGIST
KYLE MILLS, CHEF

Many cocktails owe their life to bootleg gin, the homemade swill of its Prohibition-era America, when bartenders used a creative range of ingredients to mask its grim taste. When gin was mixed with honey and lemon, someone called it "the bee's knees," the flapper generation's slang expression for "top notch" or "high quality." In this updated Bee's Knees, the accent of lavender connects the drink to the dessert.

LAVENDER BEE'S KNEES

MAKES 1 SERVING

Honey is the cocktail's hidden strength, adding a greater depth of flavor than a standard simple syrup. What makes it so refreshing is the interplay of sweet and sour (adjust the ratio of honey syrup and lemon juice to suit individual taste). "The single fresh lavender sprig as garnish adds a lovely subtle floral aroma to the drink," explains the drinksmith. "If you would like more lavender, add a few drops of lavender bitters for another layer of flavor."

★ ★ ★ ★ ★

1 ½ ounces gin
1 ½ ounces lavender-honey syrup*
½ ounce freshly pressed lemon juice
1 sprig fresh lavender

Combine gin, lavender-honey syrup, and lemon juice with ice in a shaker. Shake vigorously and strain into an old-fashioned glass over fresh ice. Garnish with lavender sprig.

*Add 1 tablespoon of dried lavender flowers to a cup of hot water and soak for at least 10 minutes. Strain into a small saucepan with 1 cup of honey. Heat to a very slow simmer, stirring to combine. Remove from heat and cool to room temperature.

LAVENDER GOAT CHEESE TARTLETS

MAKES 6 TO 8 SERVINGS

Fresh goat cheese with sweet, mild flavor and slightly salty undertones goes so well with luscious honey, an ingredient found in both cocktail and dish. The honey-sweetened drink sips smoothly with the tartlet's savory pastry and tangy filling.

★ ★ ★ ★ ★

For the crust:

2 cups slivered almonds
½ cup arrowroot powder
⅔ cup butter (cold)
½ teaspoon salt
2 tablespoons sugar

Preheat oven to 400°F. Grind almonds in food processor to coarse meal. Add remaining ingredients and blend to combine. Press into an 8-inch tart pan with a removable rim and bake for 10 to 12 minutes. Remove from heat and let cool completely.

For the filling:

2 cups fresh goat cheese (room
temperature)
2 eggs
½ teaspoon salt
2 tablespoons dried lavender flowers
3 tablespoons honey

Blend goat cheese, eggs, and salt in a food processor until well combined. Spread over crust in the tart pan, sprinkle tart with lavender flowers (rub between fingers as you sprinkle to release oils), and place in 350°F oven. Continue baking until filling and crust are pale golden, about 20 minutes. Cool tart in pan on a rack and remove rim. Drizzle with honey just before serving.

SMOKED PEACH MANHATTAN
PAIRED WITH
SOUTHERN PEACH COBBLER

◆

CRAVE DESSERT BAR, CHARLOTTE, NC
CLINT MEDLOCK, MIXOLOGIST
ANDRES ARBOLEDA, CHEF

On the subject of peaches, Alice Walker wrote, "Life is better than death, I believe, if only because it is less boring, and because it has fresh peaches in it;" and George DuMaurier concurred: "An apple is an excellent thing—until you have tried a peach!" Peaches, whiskey, and cobbler scream Southern charm and tradition. The pairing at Crave highlights the versatility of the peach and its ability to create tantalizing balance between a sweet dish and savory drink.

SMOKED PEACH MANHATTAN

MAKES 1 SERVING

A version of Jack Daniels put through charcoal filtration (known as the Lincoln County process), Gentleman Jack displays aromatics of honeysuckle and toasted oak with palate notes of vanilla, corn, and spiced honey. Additionally flattered by flavors of apricot and peach, the mellow whiskey-based cocktail is crafted to pair with a pleasing and humble dessert.

★ ★ ★ ★ ★

2 ounces Gentleman Jack Tennessee Whiskey
1 ounce apricot brandy
1 ½ ounces smoked peach simple syrup*
sprig of thyme, for garnish

Combine all ingredients in a mixing glass filled with ice. Shake vigorously and strain into a pre-chilled martini glass. Garnish with the sprig of thyme.

*Cut 4 peaches in half and remove pits. Place flesh-up on a wood-fired grill in a warm (but not hot) area of the grill until tender and juicy, about 30 minutes. Remove the skins, place in a food processor, and purée. Combine purée with 1:1 ratio of simple syrup.

SOUTHERN PEACH COBBLER

MAKES 4 SERVINGS

No matter where cobbler originated, the South has perfected this homey dessert. Baked until the peaches are tender and the golden topping sinks into the fruit and soaks up its juices.

★ ★ ★ ★ ★

½ cup butter
1 cup water
1 cup granulated sugar
2 pounds peaches, freshly skinned, pitted, and sliced
1 cup milk
1 cup all-purpose flour
1 tablespoon baking powder
¼ teaspoon kosher salt

Preheat oven to 350°F. Melt butter in an 8x10-inch baking pan. In a heavy bottom sauce pan, bring peaches, 1 cup of sugar, and 1 cup of water to a boil. Lower to simmer for 5 minutes. Turn off heat and set aside. In a mixing bowl, combine flour, milk, baking powder, and salt. Place the fruit mixture on top of the melted butter in the pan. Spoon batter evenly over the fruit mixture. Bake for 30 minutes. Serve warm out of the oven.

THE LONELY HUNTER

PAIRED WITH

CHOCOLATE-BANANA-NUT TRIFLE

HOTCHOCOLATE RESTAURANT & DESSERT BAR, CHICAGO, IL
LUKE LEFILES, MIXOLOGIST
MINDY SEGAL, CHEF

One of the oldest and most sophisticated cocktails, the whiskey-based Manhattan is subject to considerable variation and innovation—in other words, it's a cocktail that takes well to tinkering. Instead of serving the cocktail and dessert as bookends to a meal, the HotChocolate collaborators have pooled resources to create a playful and opulent pairing.

THE LONELY HUNTER

The Manhattan was the first cocktail to use vermouth as a modifier, and it is with the vermouth that Mr. LeFiles makes his statement. As a stand-alone component, Carpano Antica would provide sweetness and a hint of herbs to the rye-forward drink. Yet, once infused with the warming spices of chai, the formula transforms, softening harsh edges and adding layers of flavor.

★★★★★

1¾ ounces Old Overholt or other rye whiskey
1 ounce chai-infused Carpano Antica or other Italian vermouth*
¼ ounce simple syrup
2 dashes Angostura bitters
cinnamon stick
lemon peel medallion

Fill a rocks glass two-thirds with ice. Build cocktail over ice and stir for 30 seconds with a cinnamon stick, then discard cinnamon stick. Squeeze lemon peel over the surface to express oils and drop into the cocktail.

*Add 2 bags of spiced chai tea to a sealable jar with 1 cup of sweet vermouth and allow to steep for 2 hours.

CHOCOLATE-BANANA-NUT TRIFLE

MAKES 12 SERVINGS

Ms. Segal is a fan of unconventional combinations, and her trifle finds camaraderie with Mr. Lefiles' Manhattan, a liquid "layer cake" in its own right. The pairing delivers a complex progression of compatible, integrated flavors, beginning with earthy, fruity, nutty notes of the trifle, then, with each sip of the drink, grainy rye flavors, jammy/spice impressions, and herbal aromatics.

★ ★ ★ ★ ★

For the cashews:

nonstick vegetable oil spray
1 pound bittersweet chocolate, melted
2 cups unsalted cashews or other nuts,
toasted

Pour melted chocolate over toasted cashews in medium bowl; stir until nuts are coated with chocolate. Spread mixture onto baking sheet sprayed with nonstick vegetable oil spray. Cover with plastic wrap; refrigerate until firm, about 2 hours. Chop into bite-size pieces. Reserve ¼ cup for garnish.

For the meringue:

nonstick vegetable oil spray
1 cup unsalted cashews or other nuts,
toasted
¼ cup + ⅓ cup sugar
½ teaspoon unsweetened cocoa
6 large egg whites

Preheat oven to 275°F. Finely grind cashews, ¼ cup of the sugar, and cocoa in food processor. Beat egg whites in bowl of electric mixer on medium speed until soft peaks form. Slowly add remaining ⅓ cup sugar. Turn machine to high; beat until meringue is glossy and stiff, 2 to 3 minutes. Fold nut mixture into the meringue. Line baking sheet with parchment paper sprayed with non-stick vegetable oil spray. Spread meringue mixture onto parchment to ½-inch thickness. Bake until firm and crisp, 30 to 40 minutes. Cool completely on wire rack. Break into bite-size pieces, reserving some for garnish. (May be prepared a day or two in advance and stored in airtight container.)

For the chocolate mousse:

9 ounces bittersweet chocolate, melted
⅓ cup very hot water
1 container (12 ounces) frozen
nondairy whipped topping, thawed

Stir together melted chocolate and hot water in medium bowl until mixture is completely smooth. Cool to room temperature. Fold whipped topping into chocolate mixture. Cover; refrigerate until set, about 2 hours.

To assemble trifle:

chocolate-covered cashews (from
above)
meringue (from above)
chocolate mousse (from above)
4 or 5 ripe but firm bananas, sliced
¼-inch thick

Spread layer of chocolate-covered cashews over bottom of trifle bowl. Top with layers of meringue pieces, mousse, and banana. Repeat layering until bowl is full, ending with layer of mousse. Cover; refrigerate 2 hours or overnight. Just before serving, decorate top with reserved meringue and chocolate-covered nuts.

Bela Lugosi's Dead and Orange-Cardamom-Chocolate Financier

BELA LUGOSI'S DEAD
PAIRED WITH
ORANGE-CARDAMOM-CHOCOLATE FINANCIER

LA BELLE VIE, MINNEAPOLIS, MN
JOHNNY MICHAELS, MIXOLOGIST
DIANE YANG, PASTRY CHEF

Hungarian-born Bela Lugosi devoted thirty years to playing Dracula on the screen and was buried costumed as the Transylvanian Count (he didn't wake up at moonrise). In 1979, an English rock band called Bauhaus recorded a musical homage called "Bela Lugosi's Dead," later featured in the cult vampire film *The Hunger*. The song's title fits the cocktail," says the drinksmith, "since it is driven by the Hungarian liqueur and is finished with a robust, Hungarian blood-red wine—mirroring palate textures of the dessert."

BELA LUGOSI'S DEAD

MAKES 1 SERVING

It's an expression of mood and tones. The bounty of cherry and sweet fruit flavors in the Zwack and sweet herbal notes in the Amaro elevate the sugar level of the dry, wine-based cocktail, allowing tannins to find accord with the chocolate. The Allspice Dram adds a whisper of cinnamon, nutmeg, and cloves, and bitters ends the experience on a high note.

★ ★ ★ ★ ★

1 ounce Zwack liqueur
1 ounce Luxardo Amaro Abano
2 dashes St. Elizabeth Allspice Dram
1 dash Angostura Bitters
2 ounces Egri Bikavér or other red wine

Build ingredients in a Bordeaux glass and serve at room temperature.

ORANGE-CARDAMOM-CHOCOLATE FINANCIER

MAKES 12 FINANCIERS

The name financier is derived from its traditional rectangular mold which resembles a bar of gold. A distinctive ingredient in the recipe is *beurre noisette*, or brown butter, which contributes a nutty note to the complexity of chocolate, all the more reason for serving alongside the boldly flavored wine cocktail with concentrated fruit notes.

★ ★ ★ ★ ★

nonstick vegetable oil spray
9 tablespoons unsalted butter
1 ⅛ ounces bittersweet chocolate, finely chopped
¼ cup + 1 tablespoon all-purpose flour
1 cup powdered sugar
1 teaspoon ground cardamom
zest of 1 orange
4 egg whites

Preheat the oven to 350°F. Coat a financier mold or small muffin tin with nonstick vegetable oil spray and place on a baking sheet. Brown the butter over medium-low heat, stirring often, until it reaches a toasty, hazelnut color. Set aside. Melt the chocolate in a double boiler over low heat and keep warm. In a large bowl, whisk together flour, sugar, and cinnamon. Slowly add the egg whites and orange zest, making sure to stop and scrape the sides of the bowl. Strain the melted butter over the mixture and stir to combine, then stir in the melted chocolate. Pour the batter into the molds and bake until cakes slightly bounce back, about 15 minutes. Remove from the oven and let cool for 10 minutes. Remove cakes from molds. Serve warm or at room temperature.

ELEPHANT FLIP

PAIRED WITH

CRÈME FRAÎCHE CHEESECAKE

VITAE, NEW YORK, NY
DANIEL BRANCUSI, MIXOLOGIST
GENEVIEVE MELI, CHEF

This is, to be sure, a conceptual pairing, but the concept is both simple and sensible. In an egg-based cocktail that dates to the nineteenth century, the froth on a well-shaken flip provides a sultry feel as soon as it hits your mouth. Enriched with heavy cream and honey, the drink shares attitude and alchemy with the cheesecake's combination of cream cheese, goat cheese, and crème fraîche.

ELEPHANT FLIP

MAKES 1 SERVING

Bourbon has a woody, almost nutty taste, and since the egg tempers a fair amount of the whiskey's fire, Mr. Brancusi ramps up the flavor with roasted peanuts. Shake the drink hard and fast. It's important to mix the egg up well. "The egg adds texture, not taste," says the drinksmith, "just enough body and froth to harmonize with the cake." Nutmeg adds considerably to the aromatics of the drink.

★ ★ ★ ★ ★

1 ½ ounce roasted peanut–infused bourbon*
¾ ounce heavy cream
¾ ounce honey syrup**
1 egg yolk
nutmeg

Add bourbon, heavy cream, honey syrup, and egg yolk to a shaker and dry-shake (shake without ice). Add ice and shake again until well chilled. Strain into pre-chilled coupe. Lightly dust with freshly grated nutmeg.

*For the infused bourbon: Add 1 cup of unsalted roasted peanuts to 750 milliliters of bourbon. Let sit for three days, shaking once per day. After three days, strain and run mixture through a coffee filter to remove sediment.

**For the honey syrup: Combine 1 cup of clover honey with ⅓ cup of filtered water. Heat the mixture until the honey dissolves. Allow mixture to cool, then bottle and seal.

CRÈME FRAÎCHE CHEESECAKE

MAKES ONE 9-INCH CHEESECAKE

Cheesecake is an infinitely renewable culinary resource. Beating goat cheese and cream cheese together until completely smooth gives this cake its velvety, voluptuous texture. (Using room temperature ingredients helps enormously.) The rich and tangy, almost nutty, flavor of crème fraîche makes it fluffy and complex, echoing notes in the cocktail.

★ ★ ★ ★ ★

1 ½ cups cream cheese
½ cup fresh goat cheese
½ cup sugar
1 ½ cups crème fraîche
1 teaspoon vanilla extract
¼ teaspoon black pepper
4 large eggs

Preheat the oven to 325°F. Wrap the bottom of a 9-inch springform pan with foil and place on a baking sheet. Using an electric mixer, beat the cream cheese and goat cheese until very smooth. Add the sugar and continue beating until no lumps remain. Beat in the crème fraîche, vanilla, and pepper. Beat in the eggs one at a time, scraping down the sides of the bowl between additions, until combined. Pour the mixture into the pan and bake for 10 minutes, then reduce the temperature to 250°F and bake until the cake is just set, 45 to 60 minutes. Transfer the pan to a wire rack to cool completely. Run a knife around the edge of the pan to loosen the cake from the pan.

LIST OF CONTRIBUTORS

★ ★ ★ ★ ★

Arnaud's Restaurant and French 75 Bar, New Orleans, LA

Autre Monde Café, Berwyn, IL

B&O American Brasserie, Baltimore, MD

Bar Congress, Austin, TX

Boka Restaurant + Bar, Chicago, IL

Bradstreet Craftshouse, Minneapolis, MN

Café Maude, Minneapolis, MN

Chantanee Thai Restaurant and Bar, Bellevue, WA

Church Bar, Portland, OR

Crave Dessert Bar, Charlotte, NC

Crudo, Phoenix, AZ

David Todd's City Tavern, Morristown, NJ

Ecco, Atlanta, GA

Eolo Sicilia a Tavola, New York, NY

George's at the Cove, La Jolla, CA

HotChocolate Restaurant & Dessert Bar, Chicago, IL

Interstate Kitchen & Bar, Denver, CO

Irving Street Kitchen, Portland, OR

La Belle Vie, Minneapolis, MN

Legume Bistro/Butterjoint, Pittsburgh, PA

Local 11 Ten, Savannah, GA

Local, Norman, OK

Longman & Eagle, Chicago, IL

Meat & Potatoes, Pittsburgh, PA

Merchant, Madison, WI

Mistral Kitchen, Seattle, WA

Mooo Restaurant, Boston, MA

Moshi Moshi Sushi, Seattle, WA

Mud Hen Tavern, Los Angeles, CA

Parlor Market, Jackson, MS

Péché, Austin, TX

Picca, Los Angeles, CA

Rosebud, Altanta, GA

Rye on 3rd, Eugene, OR

Tabard Inn, Washington, DC

TASTE Restaurant & Bar, Seattle, WA

Tavern on South, Indianapolis, IN

The Cocktail Club, Charleston, SC

The Cowgirl, Sante Fe, NM

The Delmonico Room (at the Hotel Fauchère), Milford, PA

The Refinery, Vancouver, BC

The Social Club, Miami Beach, FL

Vanity Supper Club, Providence, RI

Vitae, New York, NY

ACKNOWLEDGMENTS

★ ★ ★ ★ ★

It's undeniably nice to have an assignment such as this one, and undeniably true that it would not have been possible without the help of many people.

Recipes shared herein represent the collaborative efforts of culinary artisans in forty-four of the country's most progressive and innovative kitchens and bars. Our thanks go in full measure for their generous contributions.

Thanks for the courtesies of Christine Tully Aranza, Melissa Scaramucci, Scott Walker, Chris Hannah, John Lerfald, Vajra Stratigos, Diane Yang, Chad Philips, John Sierchio, Chaim Rubenstein, Kate Connor (The Reynolds Group), Allison Ford (Green Olive Media), Melissa Broussard (Broussard Communications), Carrie DeVries (Deveney Communications), Ellen Marchman (Get Ink PR), Nathan Hambley (FRAUSE), and Elise Friemuth (PMK*BNC).

We are grateful to photographers Andrew Cebulka (The Cocktail Club), James Camp (Rosebud), Collin Andrew (Rye), Ryan Tanaka (Mud Hen Tavern), and Joice Barnard (TASTE).

Our appreciation to Kelsie Besaw and Amy Li of Skyhorse Publishing for their skillful editorial maneuvers and to Francis Liaw and Juliet Turback for enthusiasm and support. This book is not only about the art of collaboration; it was also conceived and produced in a resourceful joint effort. Special thanks to our mutual friend Barbara Lang for putting the two of us together.

Julia Hastings-Black
Michael Turback

ABOUT THE AUTHORS

★ ★ ★ ★ ★

Julia Hastings-Black has been working her way around the food world for more than a decade. As a cook, gardener, recipe tester, and culinary instructor, she is fascinated by the intersection of food and language. This is her first book.

For nearly three decades, **Michael Turback** combined inventiveness, passionate cooking with local ingredients, and an award-winning list of regional wines at his legendary Ithaca, New York, restaurant. As an author, he has previously taken on, with distinction, such single topics as the ice cream sundae, the banana split, hot chocolate, mocha, coffee drinks, progressive gin cocktails, Finger Lakes wine country, and the bounty of both the Ithaca Farmers Market and the historic North Market of Columbus, Ohio.

MY PAIRING IDEAS

MY PAIRING IDEAS

MY PAIRING IDEAS

MY PAIRING IDEAS

MY PAIRING IDEAS

MY PAIRING IDEAS

MY PAIRING IDEAS

MY PAIRING IDEAS

MY PAIRING IDEAS